THE SMART CLIENT: HOW TO WORK WITH LAWYERS AND WIN

The Handbook Every Lawyer Wishes Their Clients Had Read First

By Randy Bateman

This publication is intended for general information only and does not constitute legal advice. Reading this book does not create an attorney–client relationship. Readers should consult a licensed attorney regarding legal matters specific to their circumstances.

Published by:
Independently Published
Portland, Oregon, USA
www.BatemanLegacy.com

Printed in the United States of America
First Edition: 2026
ISBN (Paperback): 9798241319647
Cover design: Randy Bateman

DEDICATION

For Patty—my wisest counsel, my sharpest critic, my most genuine north star, and absolutely my favorite person to argue with. No one debates with more grace, humor, or uncanny ability to be right, even when she absolutely shouldn't be. She keeps me humble and honest.

For Ed Davis, my loyal Welsh Terrier, who sits beside me as I pound the keys of my computer, offering silent judgment, moral support, and the occasional reminder that it's time for a walk—usually right when I'm on a roll.

My inspiration to pursue a career in the law was my great-grandfather, John H. Beavers, a Winnsboro, Texas, attorney, East Texas judge, and—during one memorable season—a candidate for the United States Congress from Texas's Third District. Long before electronic billing or client portals existed, my great-grandfather built a reputation as one of the most respected members of the Wood County bar, the kind of man newspapers called "Judge Beavers," as if no further introduction was needed. Several volumes of Texas law reporters that once sat behind him in his chambers and then on my great-uncle's law office shelves. Now they reside in glass cases in my living room—I always looked at them in awe. A framed photograph of him at his desk watches over the desk where I write, offering a level stare that reminds me to do better work or at least avoid embarrassing the family name. If anything in these pages is wise, I credit him. If anything is foolish, I assume he briefly looked away.

I also dedicate this book to my great-uncle, Everett Beavers, the son of Judge Beavers, who carried the family profession into the next generation and practiced law in Winnsboro with the kind of steady dignity small towns never forget. While others inherited ranches, railroads, or general stores, Everett inherited the law itself—along with a library of books heavy enough to injure a man and serious enough to shape one. Where Judge Beavers offered thunder, Everett offered precision; where one made headlines, the other made clients quietly grateful. Together, they formed a small but mighty Beavers legal dynasty in East Texas, and any good sense I possess about lawyers began with the two of them.

INTRODUCTION

This book teaches you how to work with lawyers efficiently, avoid unnecessary legal fees, and dramatically improve the outcome of your case—using insider strategies lawyers use every day.

It is for everyone who has ever sat across from a lawyer—nervous, hopeful, confused, overwhelmed, or quietly calculating how much the conversation was going to cost—and for every lawyer who has sat across from a client feeling *precisely* the same way (plus wondering where their pen went, why the printer chose this moment to jam, and whether anyone on either side of the table genuinely understands the word "retainer").

QUICK START: THE 10 RULES SMART CLIENTS FOLLOW

1. Get organized early.
2. Communicate clearly.
3. Don't send emotional emails.
4. Keep everything in one folder.
5. Ask, "What's the goal?"

6. Ask, "What's the risk?"
7. Ask, "What changed?"
8. Manage emotions, not just facts.
9. Never share your case on social media.
10. Stay flexible—strategy changes.

HOW TO USE THIS BOOK

- Read it straight through, or jump to the chapter that matches your issue.
- Use the checklists at the back when preparing for meetings.
- Review the timelines and tools to reduce your legal costs.
- Use the sample emails to communicate like a pro.

THE CLIENT BILL OF RIGHTS

As a client, you have the right to:

1. Clear communication
2. Honest explanations about risks and outcomes
3. Fair billing and detailed invoices
4. Timely responses
5. Respect and professionalism

6. A strategic plan you understand
7. Copies of everything in your file
8. Full confidentiality
9. Control over major decisions
10. The right to change lawyers if needed

You're not a passenger—you're a partner.

CHAPTER ONE:

THE LAWYER MYTH—WHY WE THINK LAWYERS FIX EVERYTHING

"Ninety percent of the practice of law is common sense."—**Justice Oliver Wendell Holmes Jr**.

Most people don't call a lawyer on a good day. They call when something in their life has slipped out of place—a business deal feels wrong, a letter arrives that tightens their chest, a relationship turns confrontational, or a mistake suddenly carries consequences. In that moment, even the most capable adults feel the same quiet fear: *What do I do now? And how do I keep this from getting worse?*

The irony is that the first steps matter most. The way you prepare, communicate, and organize yourself before the lawyer ever speaks a single word can change the trajectory of your entire case. Smart Clients aren't born—they're prepared. The difference between panic and control is usually one good decision made early.

This chapter gives you that early advantage. It teaches you how to think like a lawyer's smartest client before your first meeting even begins.

The truth is simple: Smart Clients don't know the law—they know how to prepare. They ask better questions, provide better information, and understand their role long before the first billable minute ever appears. This chapter shows you exactly how to do that. It gives you the mindset and tools lawyers wish every client had on day one, so your legal matter starts with clarity, control, and confidence.

You don't need legal training to be an exceptional client. You only need to know what matters most in those first critical steps—and that begins here. By the end of this chapter, you'll understand what lawyers need from you on day one—and the simple steps that make you the most prepared person in the room. You're already ahead of most clients simply by reading this.

A good lawyer isn't a magician and definitely not a mechanic. A good lawyer is a strategist—part chess player, detective, negotiator, translator, and, depending on the day, therapist. We don't swoop in and erase a problem. We help *you* navigate it.

Clients often come in acting like passengers in their own legal lives. They slide a stack of papers across the desk, sit back, and wait for the miracle. They assume we can take any mess—missing documents, bad timing, contradictory facts—and carve it into a courtroom masterpiece. After all, Perry Mason did that in every episode. That expectation has caused more headaches than the worst lawyers you've ever heard of or read about.

There's a wide gap between what clients think lawyers do and what lawyers actually can do. Many people assume lawyers can fix everything, predict outcomes with certainty, and somehow force the other side into submission. In reality, lawyers can't create evidence out of thin air, and can't guarantee a victory. I've told plenty of clients that even in a dream case—perfect facts, perfect law, perfect courtroom—the best prediction of a win is still only about an 80%. Judges and jurors are human, and humans are unpredictable even as legal scholars preach otherwise. Mark Twain once quipped:

"A lawyer with his briefcase can steal more than a hundred men with guns." It's a joke, sure—but it's also a reminder that law is a human system, run by imperfect humans, and nothing human is ever guaranteed.

Clients assume that if we win, well, the lawyer should have—*of course*. And if the lawyer loses, it must be the lawyer's fault. This lopsided logic explains why trial lawyers age like avocados left on a sunny windowsill. I would show clients the books lining my office walls, containing reported court cases (yes, that was before the Internet age), and explain that in every case, there was only one winner and one loser, and that both sides went to trial confident of a win. I would tell them it was sobering to think that fifty percent of the time, one party lost, and there was no guarantee their odds were any better.

One day a man barged into my office, furious, clutching a stack of papers. "Fix this today," he demanded, dropping the pile upside down on my desk. Inside, I found an HOA violation, a dentist bill from years earlier, a neighbor's complaint about a barking dog, a coupon for a pizza place that had closed, and a court summons he had never bothered to open. "What exactly am I fixing?" I asked. "That's why I hired you," he replied. "You tell me." That, right there, is the reason this book was born.

A Smart Client approaches the legal process as a partnership, not a handoff. They bring the facts, the documents, the timeline, and a dose of realism. Then they work with the lawyer to build a plan that actually stands a chance. Smart Clients tell the truth, even if it makes them squirm. They respond promptly. They keep calm. They ask good questions. They know when to talk and when to stop talking. They understand that law is less about magic and more about discipline and preparation.

I entered law school fearful that I would not measure up and that I would not be able to conquer the challenging coursework ahead. I learned early on that it was not difficult at all. It was all about time and attention. If you spent enough time, *which was a lot*, and paid attention to what you were learning, *which was not easy with minimal sleep*, you could sail through and land on your feet. My experience is the same for the practice of law.

Preparing for your first meeting with a lawyer is not about perfection—it's about control. When you bring clarity, structure, and a sense of purpose into the room, everything changes. Your questions become sharper. Your lawyer's guidance becomes more precise. The entire relationship moves from uncertainty to direction.

Most clients walk into a law office hoping for reassurance. Smart Clients walk in with information, priorities, and a clear understanding of what they want to accomplish. Lawyers notice the difference immediately. They lean in more. They ask better questions. They give better advice. Strong preparation doesn't just save time and money—it strengthens your position from the first minute of the conversation.

No one can eliminate the stress of a legal problem, but you can choose how you show up for it. The steps you take now—defining your goals, organizing your facts, preparing your questions—set the tone for your entire case. Smart Clients never wait for clarity to arrive. They create it.

Once you understand your role as a prepared, engaged client, the next surprise often comes quickly: the legal process itself doesn't behave the way people expect. Cases don't move in straight lines. Progress doesn't always make noise, and some of the most critical work your lawyer does happens quietly, behind the scenes, long before anyone files a motion or steps into a courtroom. To work effectively with a lawyer, you need more than preparation—you need a basic understanding of the system your case is moving through. That's where we're headed next. In Chapter Two, we'll pull back the curtain on the hidden machinery behind every legal case, so you stop mistaking silence for failure and start recognizing strategy when you see it.

CHAPTER TWO:

THE HIDDEN SYSTEM BEHIND EVERY LEGAL CASE

This chapter explains the realities of how lawyers work behind the scenes—and why understanding those realities will save you stress, money, and frustration throughout your case.

"Justice may be blind, but she has very sophisticated systems to feel her way forward."—**Unknown**.

Most first-time clients believe legal cases unfold in a straight line: something happens, a lawyer steps in, the truth emerges, and justice moves down a clean, well-lit path. If only it were that simple. If the legal world were really that tidy, most lawyers would sleep better, bill less, and probably live five years longer.

Every legal case lives inside an invisible system—shaped by deadlines, procedures, personalities, strategy, paperwork, and timing. Lawyers spend far more time navigating this maze than they do arguing about the law itself. The law is the tip of the iceberg; the system is everything under the waterline. Ever play sports? What happens on the field is a product of countless hours of practice and preparation.

Cases are often won because the client delivered the correct information at precisely the right moment. Cases are lost when crucial facts arrive too late—or arrive stuffed into an envelope containing expired coupons and photographs of someone's cat. If you want a mental picture, think of the legal system like an airport: gates, schedules, bottlenecks, security checks, delays, paperwork, weather issues, and long stretches where nothing appears to be happening. Your lawyer is the pilot—but even the best pilot can't take off if the runway isn't clear, the tower isn't answering, or a passenger is in row 17 shouting, "Are we leaving yet?"

"*The courtroom is a battleground. Facts are your weapons.*"—**Perry Mason**.

Cases move through predictable phases:

- Information gathering
- Timeline building

- Leveraging key facts
- Filings
- Negotiation windows
- Emotional spikes
- Quiet periods
- Sudden bursts of activity
- Resolution

Clients often panic during quiet periods—convinced nothing is happening, that the case is doomed, or that the lawyer has retired and moved to Rome. But quiet is usual. Lawyers use these pauses to think, strategize, and wait for the right opening. The legal system is not Amazon Prime; nothing shows up in forty-eight hours, and if it does, it's probably a mistake.

It is challenging for a lawyer when a client is anxiously waiting for an update, but there is nothing to report. It appears the lawyer is not doing their job. The checklist system described later is of great assistance when addressing the client's anxiety.

Smart Clients trust the natural rhythm of a case. They don't panic at silence. They don't demand motion when patience is the more decisive move. They understand that, much like a good mystery novel, not every chapter involves a chase scene.

Every legal case has a story arc—setup, tension, turning points, revelations, and resolution. Lawyers read these arcs the way doctors read symptoms; experience teaches us to sense when something is brewing even when nothing appears to be moving. Understanding the system—even at a basic level—reduces stress, sharpens decision-making, and strengthens the attorney-client partnership.

If you're a fan of TV legal dramas—*Boston Legal*, *The Lincoln Lawyer*, or, for those of us with a few more miles on the odometer, *Perry Mason*—you've probably noticed a pattern. Someone hires a lawyer in the morning, and by the afternoon, they're in a packed courtroom delivering a heartfelt closing argument. It makes great television, but it has about as much to do with real legal timelines as a superhero movie has to do with physics.

In my county, the average time from filing a case to trial is about one year. In federal court, it's closer to a year and a half. And those are the cases that do make it to trial, which is the minority. Thankfully, most cases settle long before then, sparing everyone the time, expense, and blood pressure spike of a full trial.

The more you understand about the cadence of the legal system—its pauses, its silences, its moments of rapid movement followed by long stretches of waiting—the more strategic you become. Legal progress rarely looks dramatic from the outside. Most of it happens in drafts, negotiations, research, and anticipation, not in turning points or courtroom theatrics. When you stop interpreting every period of quiet as a setback, you begin to see what your lawyer sees: a long game built on timing, preparation, and patience.

Smart Clients learn the pattern. They measure progress by substance, not noise. They communicate clearly, respond promptly, stay organized, and keep their emotions steady even when the process feels still. That steadiness is not just calming—it strengthens your position more than any single document or phone call.

You cannot control the pace of the courts, opposing counsel, or the procedural rules that govern every step of your case. But you can control how you participate in the process. And when you bring patience, clarity, and strategic focus to the table, you give your lawyer the conditions they need to deliver their best work.

In the chapters ahead, you'll learn how to manage your communication, understand strategy, evaluate legal advice, and collaborate with your lawyer in ways that move your case forward. But it all begins with this: a calm understanding of how the system works—because misunderstanding it is one of the fastest and most expensive mistakes clients make.

CHAPTER THREE:

THE REAL COST OF LEGAL PROBLEMS

"The law is reason, free from passion."—**Aristotle**. (Which sounds wise until you see your first legal invoice.)

People often believe legal fees *are* the cost of a legal problem. They're not. Legal fees are just the receipt. The real price shows up elsewhere—often later, and often larger than expected. Every legal issue carries four kinds of cost:

- Financial—the invoices
- Time—the hours you'll never get back
- Emotional—the stress you carry around like a bowling ball on your chest
- Opportunity—everything in life that gets put on hold or passed up because this problem demands center stage

Seen together, these four costs explain why even a "small" legal problem rarely feels small. The invoices might be the only part you can see on paper, but time, stress, and missed opportunities are often what clients remember most when the dust settles.

One of the most expensive mistakes clients make is waiting too long to get help. Minor problems become medium problems, medium problems become full-blown crises, and crises, without exception, come with a price tag no one enjoys. Believe it or not, most lawyers do not enjoy charging clients more than necessary. Their plates are usually so full that they prefer to swiftly complete one client's work so they can quickly move on to the next.

Emotion-driven decisions are the next biggest cost. An angry client will spend money the way a tourist spends chips in Vegas: enthusiastically, impulsively, and with a look of surprise the next morning.

I handled a case for a property owner with a beautiful riverfront property. The only way to bring electricity to the property was to cross through a finite point where four properties met.

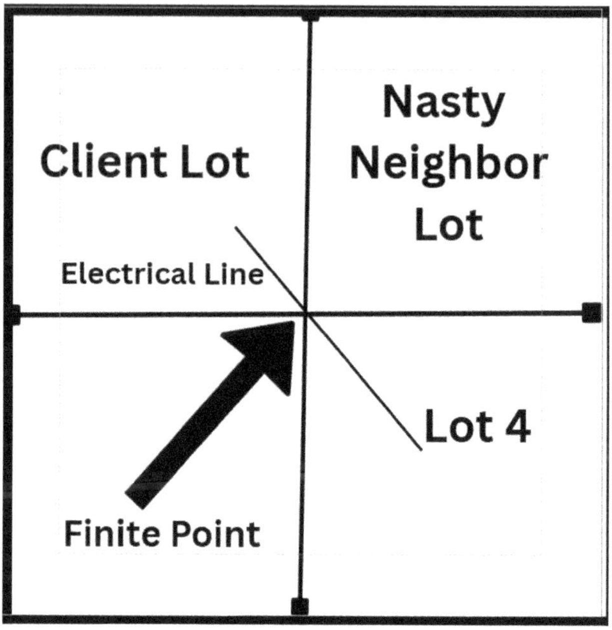

His neighbor on Lot 4 granted him an electrical easement to cross Lot 4 to reach his property. His property and the neighbor's property met at a finite point. The owner of the Neighbor Lot objected, saying you cannot make an electrical line thin enough to cross a finite point. My client installed the line, and that neighbor removed it. This went back and forth a few times. My client decided to fight fire with fire and turned in that neighbor for violations of the building code at his barn. The client finally came to see me, and I gave him the bad news that the nasty neighbor was likely right.

Nevertheless, my client wanted to go to court. We did, and lost. He owed me a tidy sum for legal fees. He said with a smile, "I will sell my lot and pay you, and I have no regrets—I couldn't give that bastard the satisfaction of me giving up without a fight." In this case, my client lost his beloved property on the river, but with his eyes wide open. His goal was very different from what mine would have been had I been in his shoes.

Some rare clients will fight regardless of the cost or the odds of winning. A lawyer needs to be abundantly clear with the client about that risk and expense. In a certain sense, lawyers appreciate these clients because they are given permission—and paid—to throw a Hail Mary. Rarely is the pass caught, but sometimes it is, and the lawyer feels like a superhero.

I was handling a complicated tax case for a doctor and his wife. They had deducted the costs of many of their personal items, such as cars, vacations, clothing, and even jewelry. It was going to be an uphill battle. We argued back and forth with the IRS agent. We made some progress, but it was not satisfactory to my clients.

I then determined that the IRS had missed the filing deadline by a single day. The IRS agent rebuffed my argument but ultimately had to concede, and my clients were not assessed a dime. A rare successful Hail Mary.

Legal stress is the cost that hides inside all the others. It steals sleep, focus, patience, productivity, connection, and joy. It can drain a week of energy in a single afternoon. Smart Clients don't pretend the stress isn't there; they manage it by staying organized, asking clear questions, and keeping their legal problem in proportion to the rest of their life.

In the end, the real expense of a legal problem isn't just what you pay your lawyer, it's everything the problem quietly steals if you let it. When you act early, make decisions with your eyes open, and choose where you want your time, money, and energy to go, you stop letting the problem run your life. You start treating it like a critical project among many, not the center of your universe.

The next chapter shows you how to do precisely that: prepare in a way that lowers every category of cost—

financial, time, emotional, and opportunity—before the meter starts running faster than you expect.

CHAPTER FOUR:

HOW TO PREPARE LIKE A PRO

Most clients don't realize how much power they hold before a lawyer ever lifts a pen. Preparation might not feel dramatic, but it determines everything: the speed of your case, the clarity of your strategy, and the size of your bill. When clients arrive organized, focused, and ready, the entire legal process accelerates. When they don't, even simple matters become scavenger hunts. This chapter shows you how to prepare in a way that gives you control, saves money, and makes your lawyer silently grateful the moment you walk through the door.

"By failing to prepare, you are preparing to fail."— **Benjamin Franklin**.

Preparation is the single biggest money-saving tool in the legal world. Not elaborate binders, color-coded tabs, or Pinterest-worthy organization—just clarity. Clarity is the one legal skill you don't need a law degree to master, yet it has a bigger impact on your legal bill than anything your lawyer does.

My longtime mentor in the legal profession was a true artist with the pen. He was Jewish, and he was denied access to most large firms after graduating from law school *magna cum laude* and earning the highest score on the bar exam. He joined his uncle and started a firm with him. They eventually hired me out of law school, even though I looked twelve at the time (so they told me later). One of the most valuable lessons he ever taught me was that when I was writing a legal document, I was doing it all wrong if my mother couldn't pick it up and understand it easily.

When clients prepare well in an organized and straightforward way, lawyers think and work faster, and bill less. When clients prepare poorly, lawyers transform—unwillingly—into detectives, therapists, investigators, archivists, and translators. And yes, all of those roles end up billed at lawyer rates, which is fun for no one.

I once had a client arrive with a slim binder labeled like a museum exhibit and a crisp one-page timeline. Her case took half the expected time, and the only thing more impressive than her preparation was her complete lack of drama.

Another client arrived with 147 unlabeled screenshots, three of which were memes he meant to send to a friend, one of which was a photo of his cat wearing sunglasses. His case cost five times as much, mainly because we spent the first two hours playing “Where’s Waldo?” with his evidence.

Great preparation isn’t complicated—it just requires intention. Clients often think lawyers want binders worthy of a Senate hearing. They don’t. They want structure, clarity, and enough organization to see the real story without digging through digital clutter. If you’re going to prepare like someone who instantly makes their lawyer’s life easier, here’s the formula:

- Write a one-page timeline.
- Gather your documents.
- Label everything—and I mean everything.
- Identify your goals.
- Write down your questions.

Preparation isn't about perfection. It's about giving your lawyer a fighting chance to solve the problem without having to sift through digital confetti to find the facts. A well-prepared client isn't just efficient—they're compelling, unstoppable, and frankly, unforgettable.

This book is for people who want to become those clients—the ones lawyers respect, judges appreciate, and opposing counsel quietly dread. It just takes time and attention.

Part of preparing for a case is sharing with opposing counsel all of the documents you intend to introduce into evidence at the trial or hearing. I had a nervous client, and we assembled all of his documents and sent them to the opposing counsel. As I prepared for trial, I organized each document in a notebook in the order I intended to use them, added an index, and labeled tabs. After the opening arguments, I handed a copy to the judge and a copy to opposing counsel. Opposing counsel immediately jumped to his feet and loudly complained that we were blindsiding them by presenting documents they had never seen. I calmly explained to the judge and opposing counsel that these were the exact same documents we had produced months ago, now just organized into a binder. It didn't reflect well on him, and we scored points with the judge. We were victorious. Preparation trumps everything else.

See Appendix A for templates and worksheets.

Preparation creates structure, but structure alone doesn't guarantee calm. Even the most organized client—timeline in hand, documents labeled, goals clearly defined—can feel their chest tighten when an unexpected email arrives, or a threatening letter lands in the mailbox. Preparation gives you leverage, but fear has a way of slipping past logic when the stakes feel personal. That's not a failure of discipline or intelligence—it's human. And it's precisely why the next skill every Smart Client must master has nothing to do with paperwork and everything to do with psychology. In the next chapter, we'll look at why legal panic takes over so quickly—and how to keep it from driving decisions you'll later regret.

CHAPTER FIVE:

THE PSYCHOLOGY OF LEGAL PANIC

Legal panic doesn't arrive politely. It hits with the force of a slammed door—sudden, loud, and impossible to ignore. Even steady, successful people who handle everyday stress with grace can find themselves spiraling when a legal threat appears. That reaction is not weakness; it is biology. This chapter explains what legal panic really is, why it takes over so quickly, and how Smart Clients learn to regain control before fear derails the strategy.

"Fear is a reaction. Courage is a decision."—**Winston Churchill**. (A helpful reminder at the exact moment your brain is trying to set itself on fire.)

Legal panic is unlike any other kind of stress. It doesn't creep in quietly. It doesn't give a polite knock. It barges in without knocking. All it takes is a single email, a letter, a phone call, or a document you weren't expecting—and suddenly your heart rate spikes, your mind starts racing, and you begin imagining outcomes that haven't happened and probably never will. Even smart, organized people—the kind who color-code their calendars and alphabetize their spice racks—experience legal panic. Why? Because legal danger feels existential. It wakes up the most primitive parts of the brain.

The Psychology Behind Legal Panic

Understanding panic begins with understanding the brain. When facing legal problems, people experience:

- Loss of control—someone else is making moves you can't predict
- Uncertainty—the process is confusing and the timeline unclear
- Threat to stability—money, reputation, relationships, and future plans feel vulnerable
- Fear of judgment—not just legally, but socially and personally

The human mind hates uncertainty more than it hates bad news. That's why a pending lawsuit often feels scarier than an actual judgment. The 'unknown' creates a vacuum—and the brain rushes to fill that vacuum with the worst-case scenario.

Fight, Flight, and the Legal System

When panic hits, most clients fall into one of two categories:

- *The Overreactor*—firing off emails, demanding action, calling repeatedly
- *The Avoider*—shutting down, ghosting the lawyer, ignoring deadlines

Both reactions make emotional sense. Neither will help your case. Lawyers spend a surprising amount of time managing client panic. A panicked client makes poor decisions, pursues bad strategies, and misunderstands communication. A significant portion of legal billing comes from cleaning up fear-driven actions that didn't need to happen.

How Smart Clients Defuse Panic

Smart Clients don't pretend they're fearless. They refuse to let the fear run the show. Here are the tools they use:

1. The 24-Minute Rule

When panic hits, wait 24 minutes before taking action. Not 24 hours—24 minutes. Long enough for emotion to settle. Short enough to avoid delay. Most panic-driven decisions evaporate in that window.

2. The One-Page Reality Check

Write down what happened, what you fear, what is actually known, and what your lawyer has already told you. This pulls panic out of your head and onto paper, where emotion loses power and logic finally has room to speak.

3. The "What Is My Lawyer Likely to Say?" Test

Ask yourself what your lawyer would probably tell you: calmly, rationally, and without drama. Most of the time, you already know the answer.

4. Separate Emotion From Instruction

Before contacting your lawyer, ask: "What do I need them to do with this information?" If the answer is "nothing," wait. Emotion clouds strategy and costs money.

5. Anchor to the Timeline

Most panic comes from not knowing where you are in the process. Smart Clients keep a simple case timeline so they understand why things are happening—or not.

The Midnight Meltdown

A client once emailed me at 12:04 a.m. with the subject line: **"URGENT—DISASTER."** He had received a strongly worded letter from opposing counsel and was convinced his life was over. The next morning, I read the letter. It was… nothing. Routine posturing. A scare tactic as old as litigation itself. But his panic cost him four hours of sleep, an entire night of rumination, and a bill for an early-morning phone consultation. Once he adopted the 24-minute rule and a case timeline, he never panicked again—even when real problems arose. His emotional steadiness became one of the most effective strategic tools in the case.

Panic is normal. Responding to panic is optional. Smart Clients don't eliminate fear—they manage it, and in doing so, they help their lawyer think clearly, work efficiently, and build stronger outcomes.

What many clients may not know is that lawyers often have the same sense of panic. They worry whether they provided poor advice to their clients, whether they have committed malpractice, whether they might be embarrassed in the courtroom, and whether their reputation in the legal community will be tarnished.

I confess I am one of those lawyers. My closest colleagues and I used to joke that we practiced law with our nerves exposed—always alert, always questioning, always a little scared. I trained myself over time not to jump to the worst conclusions and to give myself at least a day to consider the issue before responding. In more than 99% of cases, the catastrophe I imagined never arrived. Not even close. One added benefit of running scared is that I looked under every rock and questioned everything my opponents and my own clients told me, which, over the years, paid huge dividends.

In legal crises, calm isn't a personality trait—it's a strategy. It's the choice to pause, to breathe, and to respond instead of react. Panic narrows the world to a single frightening moment. Calm widens the view again so you can see the whole field—the facts, the options, the steps that actually matter.

The smartest clients don't eliminate fear; they learn how to carry it without letting it steer the wheel. They recognize that steadiness is not only good for their mental health—it directly strengthens their case. A calm client makes better decisions, asks clearer questions, communicates more effectively, and helps their lawyer do their best work.

Fear is inevitable. Panic is optional. Steadiness is learned. And once you master it, your legal life becomes far less chaotic and far more navigable.

Staying steady under pressure isn't just an internal skill—it shows up most clearly in how you communicate. Panic turns messages frantic, unfocused, and expensive. Calm turns them precise, purposeful, and valuable. Once you understand how fear hijacks decision-making, the next step is learning to speak and write in ways that protect your interests rather than undermine them. In the next chapter, we'll look at how Smart Clients communicate with their lawyers—what to say, what not to say, and how clear communication, ethical safeguards, and the attorney-client privilege work together to keep your case on track.

CHAPTER SIX:

COMMUNICATING WITH YOUR LAWYER AND THE ATTORNEY-CLIENT PRIVILEGE

Most legal problems don't fall apart because of strategy—they fall apart because of miscommunication. Clients think they explained something clearly. Lawyers believe they understand something correctly. Meanwhile, the case drifts off course because no one is actually talking about the same thing. Clear communication doesn't just help your lawyer help you; it lowers your stress, saves you money, and keeps your case from spiraling into preventable chaos.

"The single biggest problem in communication is the illusion that it has taken place."—**George Bernard Shaw**. (Every lawyer has muttered this under their breath at least once.)

Communication is the fuel of a legal case. When it's good, the whole machine runs smoothly. When it's bad, the engine coughs, sputters, and burns money faster than a vintage 1931 Ford Roadster (that I know from personal experience).

A lawyer once told me, "I don't need my clients to be perfect. I need them to be clear." It's remarkable how many legal problems survive on confusion long after the facts have dried up.

Most clients don't realize how often communication—not the law—creates the most significant problems in a case. Bad communication forces your lawyer to guess, dig, interpret, or chase down details that should have been clear from the start. Before you can communicate well, it helps to understand the habits that derail your case the fastest.

The wrong way to communicate:

- Eleven-paragraph emotional monologues
- Midnight text messages
- Forty-three forwarded screenshots with no explanation
- Calling three times in one day
- Sharing feelings instead of facts
- Failing to tell your lawyer something because you think it will hurt your case

Clear communication doesn't require legal training—it requires intention. When you give your lawyer short, factual updates, answer questions directly, and speak with purpose, you turn every interaction into forward motion. The clients who communicate well don't overwhelm their lawyers with noise; they equip them with usable information that strengthens the case.

Smart Clients communicate in a way that makes it easy for the lawyer to respond quickly, accurately, and efficiently.

They:

- Keep messages short and numbered
- Use purposeful *and updated* subject lines ("HOA dispute—timeline question")
- Understand the difference between urgent and uncomfortable
- Avoid emotional spirals (no email has ever been improved by typing while furious)
- Ask, "What do you need from me?"
- Confirm next steps so everyone stays aligned

I once had a client who saved over $3,000 simply by changing how she emailed—from constant rapid-fire micro-updates to one clear, organized summary each week. She didn't change her facts, her case, or her lawyer. She changed her communication. The savings followed.

Lawyers typically charge in six-minute increments. If you talk to your lawyer for three minutes, he or she will charge you for six. I am often asked why it costs so much for me to read a two-line email. Any guesses?

A lawyer must keep complete records, or the ship they are sailing will quickly sink when opposing counsel presents something the lawyer had but failed to maintain, or when it is critical to prosecuting a client's case. When an email or text comes in, the lawyer must acknowledge receipt, identify which case it belongs to (most lawyers are handling many cases at once, sometimes hundreds), read it, analyze how it fits into the case, and then save it electronically or save a hard copy in an organized fashion so it is not overlooked when needed for the case. I assure you, this takes more than six minutes.

Good communication turns legal chaos into a steady, predictable process—and the smoother the process, the smaller the bill.

For weekly client updates and high-stakes messages templates, see Appendix A.

*"A lawyer's first duty is loyalty—and loyalty cannot be divided."—**adapted from principles of legal ethics.***

One of the first things a competent lawyer does after you call—often before agreeing to represent you—is run a conflict check. This is not bureaucracy for bureaucracy's sake, nor is it a sign of hesitation or disinterest. It is an ethical requirement. Lawyers are prohibited from representing clients when their loyalty is divided, or even appears to be divided. If your lawyer has represented your opponent, advised someone on the other side of the transaction, or holds confidential information that could affect your matter, the rules require them to stop, check, and sometimes decline the case altogether.

From a client's perspective, conflict checks can feel oddly anticlimactic. You pour out your story, brace yourself for action—and then the lawyer says, "Let me run a conflicts check and get back to you." This is the legal equivalent of a pilot doing a pre-flight checklist. You may be eager to take off, but you should be grateful someone is making sure the wings are attached. A lawyer who skips or rushes this step is not being efficient; they are being reckless and possibly unethical.

Conflict checks also explain why the size of a law firm matters more than clients often realize. In a small firm or solo practice, the conflict check may be quick and straightforward—sometimes as simple as reviewing a short client list and a matter log. In a large firm with hundreds or thousands of lawyers, the process can involve firm-wide databases, multiple offices, affiliated entities, and historical matters stretching back decades. The upside of a large firm is breadth of experience; the downside is that clearing conflicts can take longer.

In one well-known malpractice case, a mid-size law firm agreed to represent a business owner in a commercial dispute without running a thorough conflict check. Months into the litigation—after discovery, motion practice, and significant legal fees—it emerged that another lawyer in the same firm had previously represented the opposing party in a related matter years earlier. No one remembered it. The database had not been thoroughly searched. The conflict was real.

The result was catastrophic for the client. The court disqualified the firm from continuing the case. The client had to hire new counsel, re-educate them from scratch, and attempt to salvage a strategy midstream. Worse, certain tactical decisions could not be undone, and confidential information had already been shared inside the conflicted firm. The client then sued their former lawyers for malpractice to recover the fees and the lost momentum.

This is why conflict checks are not a technicality and not an optional courtesy. They exist to prevent precisely this kind of slow-motion disaster. When a lawyer says they need time to clear conflicts, what they are really saying is: “I am making sure I can stand next to you—fully and exclusively—when this gets hard.”

The takeaway for Smart Clients is simple: don’t take offense, don’t overshare before clearance, and don’t pressure a lawyer to hurry this step. Conflict checks protect you as much as they protect the lawyer. They help ensure your lawyer’s advice is unconflicted, your confidences remain secure, and your case is not derailed months later because someone suddenly realizes, “Oh right—we represented the other side in 2012.” Few sentences in law are scarier than that one.

Clear communication and ethical alignment create the foundation—but they’re not the end of the story. Once your lawyer has the whole picture, understands your goals, and can act without divided loyalties, the focus shifts to what comes next: deciding *how* and *when* to move. Strategy is where preparation, calm, and communication finally converge. It’s the moment your case stops being a collection of facts and starts becoming a plan. In the next chapter, we’ll demystify legal strategy—not so you can practice law yourself, but so you can understand the reasoning behind the moves your lawyer recommends and participate intelligently in the decisions that matter most.

CHAPTER SEVEN:

UNDERSTANDING STRATEGY WITHOUT A LAW DEGREE

"Strategy is a system of expedients."—**Helmuth von Moltke**. (Or, as every lawyer eventually learns: no plan survives first contact with opposing counsel.)

Most clients believe strategy is the glamorous part of law—the courtroom theatrics, the dramatic cross-examinations, the surprise evidence revealed at the perfect moment. In reality, strategy is far quieter and far more deliberate. It's patience, timing, leverage, psychology, and information management. Clients often assume lawyers make strategic decisions based on gut instinct or some mystical intuition. The truth is much more methodical. Lawyers think in terms of:

- Risk
- Opportunity
- Cost
- Timing
- Probability
- Human behavior

One of the best ways to understand legal strategy is to picture a chessboard. The early moves matter. Position matters. Sometimes the smartest move on the board is not advancing—it's waiting, watching, and letting the other side reveal their intentions.

Let me give you an example of how timing—not volume—wins cases. A client once insisted we send a harsh, fiery letter to the opposing side. He wanted impact. He wanted dominance. He wanted revenge wrapped in legal stationery. But the timing was awful—the other side was emotional, reactive, and ready to ignite. Any aggressive move would have turned a minor conflict into a full-scale blaze. So we waited. Three days later, the temperature dropped, the emotions cooled, and the other side reached out asking to talk—no theatrics, no fireworks—just progress. Strategy isn't about noise. It's about results.

Here's the truth: good strategy changes. As new facts emerge, smart lawyers revise their plan. A rigid strategy isn't a strategy at all—it's wishful thinking in a suit.

Smart Clients strengthen strategy by sharing information early, staying flexible, asking, "What's the reasoning behind that move?", staying emotionally steady, and trusting the timing.

One overlooked text message can shift the entire direction of a case. One unexpected witness can turn a losing negotiation into a winning settlement. One sincere apology can defuse a whole lawsuit.

This is where our TV lawyers are instructive. They often stumble onto a last-minute witness, a missing document, or—as TV writers love—the proverbial "smoking gun." If you are rigid and not open to new information and changes in strategy, your chances of success plummet.

As a young lawyer, I spent most of my time trying cases. I always built at least one legal theory into the case that would allow an appeal to the U.S. Supreme Court if everything went sideways. I wasn't yet a member of the Federal Bar (though I later joined), but having that backup strategy kept me sharp.

I used it once in a rural courtroom where every local lawyer knew every local judge. My client's home was sold at a foreclosure auction she was never told about—the auction took place on the courthouse steps without a single notice to her. Had she known, she could have shown up and bid to buy back her own house.

When I raised a federal due-process argument, the local lawyers literally laughed out loud in open court. The judge didn't. He thought it over and ruled in our favor, forcing a new sale with proper notice. The opposing lawyers turned red with frustration, but it accomplished exactly what we needed: time and fairness.

Then the strategy took over. We prepared for the new sale by showing up with a briefcase full of cash—plus an extra $5,000 in case the bidding escalated. The vindictive family member pursuing the foreclosure didn't bring a dollar, assuming no one would challenge him. He bid. We bid $10 more. We won. The house was worth far more than the debt, and my client walked away with her home and her dignity intact.

Understanding strategy doesn't mean predicting every twist in your case. It means recognizing the forces that shape those twists—timing, leverage, psychology, and information. When you begin to see strategy the way a lawyer does, you stop expecting certainty and start expecting evolution.

Smart Clients don't push for rash moves, rigid plans, or emotional fireworks. They strengthen strategy by sharing information early, staying flexible, asking why a move makes sense, and trusting the timing even when the process feels slow. Strategy succeeds not because it's forceful, but because it adapts.

That mindset turns you from a passenger in your legal matter into a partner in its outcome. And once you learn to think strategically, every legal challenge—big or small—becomes easier to navigate.

Understanding strategy changes how you see your case—but strategy only works if the person executing it is the right fit. A brilliant plan in the wrong hands can fail just as quickly as a weak plan in the right ones can succeed. Once you understand how timing, leverage, and adaptability shape legal outcomes, the next critical decision becomes clear: choosing the lawyer whose instincts and style align with the strategy your case actually requires. In the next chapter, we'll look at how to make that choice deliberately, by understanding the three core lawyer archetypes—and why picking the wrong one can quietly derail even a well-designed plan.

CHAPTER EIGHT:

CHOOSING THE RIGHT LAWYER—THE THREE ARCHETYPES

Choosing the right lawyer is one of the most important decisions a client ever makes—and one of the most misunderstood. People assume all lawyers operate the same way, or that talent alone determines outcomes. But different lawyers approach cases with entirely different instincts, temperaments, and strategic styles. If you match the right style to the right problem, your case accelerates. If you mismatch it, even a brilliant lawyer can make everything more complicated.

"In the choice of a lawyer, as in the choice of a physician, the highest skill is worth nothing without the closest attention."—**John Ruskin**. (And legal "attention" has nothing to do with volume—and everything to do with judgment.)

Most people choose a lawyer the way they choose a restaurant on a road trip—by convenience, instinct, or panic. But choosing the right lawyer is far closer to selecting the right surgeon: the fit matters—sometimes more than the talent.

To make this simple, it helps to group lawyers by the instinctive way they solve problems—their operating style. After decades of watching lawyers in the wild, I've learned that nearly all of them fall into one of three archetypes:

- The Shark
- The Surgeon
- The Schoolteacher

Each one is brilliant in the proper context—and a catastrophe in the wrong one.

1. The Shark

The Shark is aggressive, loud, relentless, and occasionally terrifying in a way that can be very effective. They thrive in disputes where fear, pressure, and intimidation drive results. Sharks swim fast, bite hard, and negotiate like every interaction is round twelve of a heavyweight fight.

Clients love the idea of hiring a Shark because it feels like hiring a warrior. But Sharks come with side effects. They escalate conflict, inflame emotions, increase legal costs, and antagonize the other side into trench warfare.

A Shark is ideal when the other side is dishonest, the stakes are high, the situation requires force, or you need someone fearless in a courtroom.

They are not ideal when you need nuance, subtle negotiation, quiet diplomacy, or a relationship left standing when the dust settles.

2. The Surgeon

The surgeon is calm, analytical, and ruthlessly precise. They don't waste words, motions, or time. Their favorite phrase is, "What's the goal?" Surgeons win cases quietly. Sometimes so quietly that clients worry they're not doing enough—when in reality the work is happening inside their head, not in dramatic email chains.

A Surgeon is ideal when evidence matters more than emotion, strategy must be subtle, the case depends on details, and you want efficient, outcome-driven thinking.

Surgeons win in conference rooms, not courtrooms. They are the lawyers other lawyers hire when *they* get in trouble.

My mentor was the Surgeon, and the style I eventually grew into. One of my favorite clients, who stuck with me for decades, referred to me as "the velvet hammer." I wore that title as a badge of honor. My partners called me Robo Lawyer because I never let up until I had the result I wanted.

3. The Schoolteacher

The Schoolteacher is patient, warm, thorough, and remarkably good at breaking down complex ideas. They make the law understandable. They check in. They explain the "why" behind the "what." They walk you step-by-step.

They are ideal for first-time clients, emotional situations, families, estate issues, and any matter requiring compassion and clarity.

But here's the one catch: Schoolteachers can be too patient—and in legal work, excessive patience can slow momentum or soften necessary edges. I had a partner like that at one time who made clients feel great about their cases and then explained in excruciating detail all the ways the case could go badly. The clients felt informed; the outcomes often didn't match their confidence.

Archetypes aren't labels—they're tools. And they only work when you pair the right tool with the right job. The secret: *Pair the Lawyer with the Problem.* When a case called for a Shark, I referred my client to one.

A Shark is terrible for a gentle settlement. A Schoolteacher is awful for a hostile dispute. A Surgeon is horrible for a case that requires aggressive theatrics. When you align the lawyer with your actual goal, the entire case changes.

A Smart Client starts by asking:

- "What outcome do I want emotionally?"
- "What outcome do I want legally?
- "What outcome do I want financially?"
- "What outcome will matter most in five years?"

Here's a perfect example of what happens when the archetype and the problem don't match. A woman hired a feared Shark to handle her father's probate. She wanted strength, fire, and dominance. But probate is about paperwork, communication, and family diplomacy. A Shark was gasoline on a room full of candles. After months of unnecessary conflict, she switched to a Schoolteacher-style attorney. Within two weeks, the entire case calmed down. The Shark wasn't the wrong person—he was simply the wrong fit.

Choosing the right lawyer has very little to do with personality and everything to do with alignment. When you understand the archetypes, you stop hiring out of fear, urgency, or guesswork—and you start choosing based on the outcome you actually want. A Shark delivers force. A Surgeon provides precision. A

Schoolteacher delivers clarity. All three are brilliant when used correctly, but disastrous when used blindly.

Smart Clients don't ask, "Who's the most aggressive?" or "Who seems the nicest?" They ask, "Which style fits the strategy my case requires?" Once you make that shift, the entire legal process becomes calmer, clearer, and far more effective.

Use the evaluation and interview prep sheets to compare attorneys and choose the lawyer whose strengths align with your actual goals—not your fears. See Appendix A for templates and worksheets.

Once you understand which kind of lawyer your situation actually requires, the next challenge becomes practical: finding a real human who fits that profile. Knowing the archetypes prevents you from hiring the wrong style. Still, it doesn't tell you where quality actually lives—or how to separate true professional excellence from marketing, visibility, or charm. The next chapter focuses on exactly that problem: how Smart Clients locate, evaluate, and choose high-quality lawyers in the real world, before the first invoice ever arrives.

CHAPTER NINE:

HOW DO I FIND A QUALITY LAWYER?

Finding a quality lawyer isn't about luck, advertising, or hoping the first Google result is a good human being. It's about knowing what signals actually matter in the legal profession. Some lawyers impress clients; others impress judges. The smartest clients learn how to tell the difference. This chapter shows you where real quality comes from—and how to recognize it before you sign a fee agreement.

"Anyone can hold the helm when the sea is calm."— **Publilius Syrus.**

Clients sometimes ask whether they're better off with a male or female lawyer, as if the courtroom were a boxing ring with separate weight classes. The truth? Gender has about as much to do with legal skill as a judge's robe has to do with their golf swing. Some people assume male lawyers are tougher, forgetting that some of the fiercest cross-examiners on earth answer to names like Linda, Maria, or Judge Mom. Others assume female lawyers are more compassionate—until they watch one dismantle a witness so cleanly the bailiff needs a dustpan. What actually matters is whether your lawyer is smart, prepared, ethical, unflappable, and able to explain things to you without requiring a translator. Choose the brain, not the chromosomes.

Once you stop focusing on irrelevant qualities, the next step is avoiding the traps that lead many clients to the wrong lawyer.

Finding a quality lawyer is not as simple as typing a name into Google or picking the attorney whose face appears on the side of a city bus. Choosing wisely requires a blend of caution, research, and understanding the signals that actually matter in the legal profession.

Many clients start with advertising—billboards, radio spots, late-night TV commercials, and splashy Internet banners. Some of these lawyers are excellent; others simply have excellent marketing budgets. Advertising tells you that a lawyer wants clients. It does not tell you whether that lawyer is respected by judges, trusted by peers, or capable of handling a matter like yours. Use ads as introductions, not endorsements.

Bar association referral services can be a helpful next step. They will not rank lawyers for you, but they can point you toward attorneys who are licensed, insured, and practicing in the correct specialty. These referrals are designed to give the public a reliable starting place—not necessarily the most elite lawyer, but a competent one. For many everyday legal problems, that is enough.

For clients who want a deeper, more reliable measure of quality, peer-reviewed publications are some of the strongest tools available. Chambers and Partners (https://chambers.com), The Best Lawyers in America (https://www.bestlawyers.com), and Super Lawyers (https://www.superlawyers.com) all rely on evaluations from other lawyers and, in some cases, judges. Their rankings are not perfect, but they carry weight because lawyers know who consistently produces excellent work. When a lawyer appears in these publications year after year, it is rarely accidental.

Most of these organizations and groups have websites where you can search for lawyers in your state, read about them, and learn what other lawyers have to say about them. I would often use these sites to locate lawyers for clients who needed lawyers in states where I was not licensed to practice law. This was not necessary when I was at the AM Law 100 firm, but it was when I was at the smaller firms.

Some of the strongest signals of excellence come from the invitation-only legal colleges: the American College of Trial Lawyers (https://www.actl.com/), the American College of Real Estate Lawyers (https://www.acrel.org/acrel/default.asp), the American College of Mortgage Attorneys (https://www.acmaatty.org/), and the American College of Bankruptcy (https://www.americancollegeofbankruptcy.com/). Most of the other legal disciplines have similar American Colleges. These organizations do not accept applications. Members are nominated, vetted, and invited only after demonstrating exceptional skill, professionalism, and integrity. If your lawyer belongs to one of these groups, it is a meaningful signal—not of prestige alone, but of mastery.

The smartest clients blend these approaches. They start broad, narrow the list through research, and then rely on conversations, instincts, and clarity about their goals. A quality lawyer is not always the most visible one—but they are almost always the most trusted by those who genuinely know the profession.

Don't overlook the state bar association websites. On some bar websites, you can check whether any complaints have ever been filed against the lawyer. Don't hesitate to ask the lawyer about anything you find. Their reaction will tell you more than the complaint itself.

This is an extreme case—but extreme cases reveal the vulnerabilities of trust better than mild ones ever could. Tom Girardi—a famous Hollywood class-action lawyer (and inspiration for *Erin Brockovich*)—represented plane-crash victims, widows, orphans, and burn victims. For years, clients adored him because he won big settlements. Then the truth came out. Girardi had stolen millions from his own clients, used trust funds to finance a luxury lifestyle, left widows and orphans without the money owed to them, and deceived courts, clients, and partners for years. He was eventually disbarred, went bankrupt, and was criminally charged. He began his 87-month prison sentence in July of 2025. His clients never saw a dollar of what they were owed. Some are still trying to recover their money.

A lawyer's reputation is far more critical than a lawyer's promises. Skill can be advertised; trust must be earned. When you evaluate lawyers by their track record, their standing in the profession, their clarity, and their integrity, you protect yourself from the flashiest dangers in the legal world—and from the Tom Girardis who fool clients but never fool other lawyers.

A quality lawyer is someone whose work is respected where it matters: in courtrooms, conference rooms, and peer evaluations. When you learn to read those signals, you stop gambling on legal representation and start choosing it with precision.

Once you know how to recognize quality in an individual lawyer, the next layer becomes unavoidable: the environment that the lawyer works within. Skill, judgment, and integrity don't exist in a vacuum. They're shaped—for better or worse—by the structure, incentives, and resources of the firm behind the lawyer. A great attorney within the wrong-sized organization can be constrained; an average attorney within the right-sized organization can sometimes outperform expectations. In the next chapter, we'll look at how law firm size affects cost, strategy, speed, and outcomes—and how Smart Clients decide when size truly matters and when it doesn't.

CHAPTER TEN:

DOES SIZE MATTER?

When choosing a lawyer, most clients focus on personality, recommendations, or urgency. Rarely do they consider something far more influential: the size of the law firm behind the lawyer. Whether your lawyer works in a one-lawyer shop or a global powerhouse with 1,000+ attorneys matters—not because size equals quality, but because size shapes structure, cost, strategy, resources, incentives, and even how your lawyer thinks.

"A big law firm is like an aircraft carrier: impressive, powerful, and slow to turn."—**Unknown**.

This chapter is your guide to navigating that landscape like a pro. Once you understand that firm size shapes incentives and structure, the next question becomes obvious: how much does it matter for your specific case?

Why Size Matters (and Why It Sometimes Doesn't)

Law firms come in five basic forms:

- solo practitioners
- small firms (2–10 lawyers)
- mid-sized firms (10–75 lawyers)
- large firms (AM Law 100 and AM Law 200)
- boutique specialty firms (small in size, elite in focus)

Each has strengths, each has weaknesses, and each fits different clients.

THE SOLO PRACTITIONER

Pros: personal attention, flexible billing, deep relationships, and no layers of bureaucracy.

Cons: limited resources, limited staffing during emergencies, fewer specialists on hand, and cases may move more slowly.

Great for simple disputes, wills and trusts, straightforward contracts, small landlord-tenant issues, and local matters. Small firms in rural areas tend to have the upper hand because litigants from outside the region, especially from much larger cities, are distrusted by local judges and juries, and local attorneys often have more sway with those local judges and juries. *Do not underestimate this advantage.*

Not great for complex litigation, multi-party cases, urgent high-stakes disputes, and cases requiring specialized expertise. That being said, in the early 1990s, attorney Jan Schlichtmann—a Massachusetts solo lawyer—took on Philip Morris, one of the most powerful corporations in the world. He had no large staff, no corporate backing, and no safety net. What he did have was an unwavering belief that his client had been mistreated.

Philip Morris deployed full-scale corporate firepower. Schlichtmann countered with strategy, precision, and sheer grit. His cross-examinations exposed contradictions in the company's own documents, rattling a defense team that expected to steamroll him. Eventually, Philip Morris agreed to a significant confidential settlement—widely reported to be in the tens of millions—rather than risk a public verdict.

The victory became a national reminder that a small firm can sometimes outmaneuver a giant, not through size, but through focus.

THE SMALL FIRM (2–10 lawyers)

Pros: collaborative environment, lower rates, multiple lawyers without massive bureaucracy, and attorney continuity.

Cons: still limited resources, may lack deep specialization, and risk of overload if multiple cases go hot at once.

Great for: business disputes, family law, probate, employment matters, and local civil litigation.

THE MID-SIZE FIRM (10–75 lawyers)

Pros: more specialization, good support staff, access to a broader range of attorneys, strong litigation support, and balanced cost-to-talent ratio.

Cons: higher rates, some bureaucracy, and not always equipped for national-level cases.

Great for: regional litigation, complex business matters, appeals, real estate disputes, and medium- to large-scale corporate needs.

THE BIG FIRMS—THE AM LAW 100

These are the mega-firms: 500–3,000 lawyers, multi-city, sometimes multi-continent.

Pros: unmatched resources, subject-matter specialists for almost anything, deep bench strength, sophisticated teams for complex litigation, and name recognition (sometimes helpful, sometimes not).

Cons: breathtaking hourly rates, billing quotas that drive behavior, layers of staffing, partners who may touch your case far less than you expect, and corporate priorities over personal ones.

A famous anecdote describes a partner at a large Wall Street firm who billed 27 hours in a single day by flying cross-country and billing nearly every minute of travel (including the three extra hours based on the time change during the flight). Large-firm culture rewards hours, and sometimes that distorts incentives.

Great for massive civil litigation, national cases, antitrust, securities, major corporate deals, and cases where the other side hired a big firm. In these cases, legal fees are often insignificant compared to the dollar amounts at stake.

Not great for simple matters, cost-sensitive clients, and disputes where efficiency matters more than firepower. During my 18 years at an AM Law 100 firm, there were many cases we could not take because the stakes were not high enough to justify the legal fees we would have had to charge.

THE BOUTIQUE SPECIALTY FIRM

These are small teams of elite specialists—often lawyers who left big firms to focus on one area. This is precisely what I did with some trusted colleagues during the final two decades of my career. We used our expertise to form our own firm, and fortunately, all our clients followed us. Most of our clients were Fortune 500 companies, and the amounts at risk were substantial.

Pros: world-class expertise in a narrow field, lower overhead than AM Law firms, highly personalized service, and efficient teams.

Cons: limited specialties and may need to outsource unrelated issues.

Great for: intellectual property, appellate work, tax, real estate, environmental law, and high-level litigation requiring specialists.

Once you understand the strengths and limitations of each firm type, the next step is to match your case to the environment where it will succeed.

How to Choose the Right Size Firm

Ask yourself:

- How complex is my case?
- How much can I realistically spend?
- Does my case require specialized knowledge?
- Does my case require a team?
- Do I need courtroom muscle or quiet strategy?

I spent my first seven years in a small firm, my next two decades in an AM Law 100 firm, and my final two decades in a boutique specialty practice. Each one taught me something different. The big firm had resources that the smaller firms could never match. The small and boutique firms had the agility that the big firms could never offer. What mattered most wasn't the size—it was whether the firm's structure fit the problem at hand.

A small firm may win where a large firm flounders, and a large firm may overwhelm a case that a solo lawyer could handle for a fraction of the cost. Another hard-learned lesson is never to underestimate a lawyer just because they are from a small firm. Some of the most talented and crafty lawyers I dealt with were from small firms.

Once you understand how firm size shapes incentives, resources, and behavior, the final—and most decisive—step becomes personal. Structures matter, but outcomes are ultimately driven by the individual lawyer sitting across the table from you. That's where Smart Clients shift from analysis to action. The next chapter shows you how to interview lawyers the way experienced CEOs do—not as a hopeful applicant, but as a decision-maker. When you know what to ask, what to listen for, and how to evaluate judgment under pressure, you stop guessing and start choosing with confidence.

CHAPTER ELEVEN:
HOW TO INTERVIEW A LAWYER LIKE A CEO

Interviewing a lawyer is one of the most important moments in your entire legal journey—and one of the most misunderstood. Most clients think they're supposed to impress the lawyer. In reality, the lawyer should be impressing them. CEOs understand this instinctively: the person asking the questions holds the power. When you think like a CEO, you stop hoping for a good lawyer and start selecting one with intention.

"The most important thing in communication is hearing what isn't said."—**Peter Drucker.** (CEOs understand this instinctively; good lawyers do too, and when you begin thinking the way CEOs think, the entire interview changes shape.)

Most clients walk into a lawyer interview the way they walk into the DMV—nervous, confused, and silently praying they brought the proper paperwork. CEOs walk in differently. They show up clear, confident, and fully aware that *they* are the ones running the meeting.

Here's the truth most clients never hear: you are not auditioning—you are hiring. You are the employer in this relationship. You assess, evaluate, and choose, just like a CEO selecting a key advisor. Never feel embarrassed that your matter is too small or insignificant. If the lawyer you interview gives off that impression, thank them for their time and leave.

So what exactly should you be evaluating when you sit across from a lawyer? CEOs already know the answer.

What CEOs Understand That Most Clients Don't.

CEOs look for:

- Competence
- Communication style
- Strategic thinking
- Alignment with goals
- Judgment under pressure

You should do precisely the same.

Step One: Know Your Goal Before You Walk In

A lawyer can only serve a clear purpose. Before the meeting, write down:

- What outcome do I want?
- What am I afraid of?
- What's my timeline?
- What resources do I have?
- What am I willing to settle for?

Clarity = power, and lawyers can smell it.

Step Two: Ask These Five CEO-Level Questions

These five questions reveal more in fifteen minutes than an hour of polite conversation:

- "What is the most likely outcome you see based on what I've told you?" If they promise certainty, politely exit. If they talk probabilities, you may have found your lawyer.
- "What are the biggest risks in my case?" Smart lawyers start with weaknesses.

- "How do you prefer clients communicate with you?" This prevents half the misunderstandings that derail cases.
- "What is your general approach to conflict?" Listen closely—Sharks, Surgeons, and Schoolteachers all reveal themselves here.
- "If you were in my shoes, what would your first move be?" Great lawyers never hesitate. They know the terrain instantly.

Step Three: Watch for Red Flags

Red flags in a lawyer interview are like red flags on a first date—ignore them, and you'll regret it later.

Watch for:

- Constant interruptions
- Bad-mouthing other lawyers
- Guaranteed outcomes
- Rushed or distracted energy
- Fee talk without strategy talk
- No questions for you

A lawyer who never asks questions is a lawyer who will miss something important.

Step Four: Evaluate Their Fit—Not Their Theater

Some lawyers try to win clients with theatrics—booming voices, dire warnings, melodramatic speeches. Ignore every bit of it.

Focus instead on calm competence, clear logic, respectful listening, strategic precision, and emotional steadiness.

These traits win cases. Drama sells commercials.

Step Five: Ask the Money Question—Professionally

Not: *"How much will this cost?"* (They can't possibly know yet.) Instead, ask: *What factors will influence the total cost—and which of those can I control?"* This separates the real lawyers from the performers.

The Client Who Interviewed Like a Pro

A man once walked into my office with a clipboard—already a signal I needed to bring my A game. He asked concise questions, took notes, and even challenged me on two points. He wasn't being difficult; he was evaluating me. After I answered his final question, he said, "Great. I want to hire you. What do you need from me first?" We worked together for years. He was one of my best clients—not because he was wealthy or clever, but because he treated the process seriously and professionally.

I recall a time when I was sitting in the conference room of one of the most successful developers in the region. He was interviewing for new counsel after his lawyer retired. My competitors were all at the table. They dominated the conversation in the room. I asked questions and listened. At the end of the lengthy meeting, the owner announced he had made his decision and selected me. He shared that he had worked with many lawyers over the years, including some of the finest in the Pacific Northwest. He said the best quality of all to him was when a lawyer asked him about his goals and objectives and listened to him. He said it was all too common for lawyers to assume they knew more than he did and knew what was best for him. He viewed that as decision-making in a vacuum. He thanked everyone, and we worked closely together until the final day of my retirement.

A Smart Client's Guide to Lawyer Billing

Lawyers generally charge in one of four ways: hourly rates, flat fees, contingency fees, and hybrid arrangements. Hourly billing is the old warhorse of the profession—you pay for every six-minute increment the lawyer spends working on (or thinking about working on) your case. The upside is flexibility. The downside is that the meter runs fast, especially if your lawyer has strong feelings about email. Flat fees offer predictability: one price for a clearly defined project. They shine in straightforward work such as wills, business formations, and routine real estate matters. But if anything unexpected pops up, a flat fee can turn into a negotiation about what's "included"—like arguing over which toppings count as "part of the combo meal."

In late 2025, The Wall Street Journal reported what many in the legal world had long suspected: the billable hour is no longer immortal. With AI handling routine legal tasks at lightning speed—research, document review, drafting—firms can no longer justify charging clients for hours that machines now complete in minutes. The article describes a quiet but decisive shift across the industry as lawyers pivot toward value-based and subscription-style fee models, pricing their services not by time spent but by the outcome achieved and the strategic expertise the attorney brings to the relationship. For clients, this is excellent news. It means clearer expectations, fewer surprises, predictable budgeting, and a legal market finally forced to compete on efficiency and results rather than on who can bill the most hours.

Contingency fees are standard in personal injury cases, where the lawyer gets a percentage only if you win. This aligns incentives nicely, but it also means the lawyer might be very enthusiastic about settling quickly. Hybrid fee structures mix and match—for example, a reduced hourly rate plus a small contingency bonus—and can be smart when the risk and workload are hard to predict.

But hourly rates are only one piece of the cost puzzle. The rest often surprises clients. These can include court filing fees, service-of-process charges, postage and certified mailing, photocopying or scanning, long-distance phone calls, research database fees, travel time and mileage, expert witness fees, deposition transcripts, and even administrative time from paralegals or support staff. None of these charges is inherently unreasonable—many are unavoidable—but they can add up quickly if you aren't paying attention. A Smart Client asks for a written list of potential costs at the outset, understands which items are essential, and pushes back on anything that seems excessive or unexplained. At my AM Law 100 firm, our copy machines were set up to require a client number before making copies, so the copies were automatically added to a client bill. A slip of a keystroke can accidentally add a large cost to your file that was intended for a different client file.

The bottom line: no fee structure is inherently good or bad. The key is clarity. Make your lawyer explain the billing method in writing, with examples. If the explanation feels slippery, confusing, or like it belongs on the back of a cocktail napkin, that's a red flag.

"The law is a system that protects everybody who can afford to hire a good lawyer." **Mark Twain**.

Here's a modern example of how a simple legal matter can become a costly misadventure. In 2024, a Portland tech entrepreneur hired a lawyer to handle what he believed was a "simple" trademark filing. The lawyer—who billed hourly at a rate that suggested he often vacationed in Tuscany— estimated the job would take "no more than three hours." Perfect, thought the entrepreneur. Straightforward. Predictable. Affordable.

Fast-forward six weeks. The client received a 14-page invoice totaling $9,742.50, including such gems as: "Review client's email (2.4 hours)." "Consider implications of emoji in client's product name (1.8 hours)." "Internal discussion about whether avocado emoji is protected speech (3.1 hours)." When the bewildered client asked how the bill ballooned, the lawyer replied, "Well, intellectual property is complicated." The client responded, "So is my marriage after showing my spouse this invoice."

The kicker? The USPTO rejected the filing itself because of a fundamental clerical error—the same error the lawyer had billed $425 to "triple-check."

The entrepreneur now shares his story at every networking event with the moral: "Don't just hire a lawyer you like—hire a lawyer who won't need to build an addition on their house because of your case."

Include a candid billing conversation in your interview.

Interviewing your lawyer well puts you in control—but control doesn't end once the engagement letter is signed. In fact, many of the most costly mistakes happen *after* a Smart Client has chosen the right lawyer, asked the right questions, and felt confident about the relationship. That's because pressure changes behavior, even for capable, thoughtful people. The next chapter focuses on the communication traps that quietly derail cases, inflate bills, and strain relationships—not because clients are careless, but because stress makes even good habits slip. Learning to avoid these mistakes is how Smart Clients turn a strong start into a successful outcome.

CHAPTER TWELVE:

THE COMMUNICATION MISTAKES EVEN SMART CLIENTS MAKE

Even the smartest, calmest, most deliberate clients make communication mistakes. It isn't a character flaw—it's the nature of being human in a stressful situation. Legal problems distort judgment, tighten emotions, and make small details feel enormous. The good news is that most communication errors are predictable, preventable, and easy to fix once you know what to look for. This chapter shows you how to avoid the traps that quietly inflate bills, slow cases, and frustrate even the most patient lawyers.

"Confidence is a feeling, not a measure of accuracy."— **Daniel Kahneman.**

Smart Clients aren't perfect clients. Even the most organized, emotionally steady, well-intentioned people make communication errors that complicate their cases—and cost them money. The key is knowing these mistakes before they grow legs and sprint straight into chaos.

Most communication errors fall into five predictable categories:

- Over-communication
- Under-communication
- Emotional communication
- Unclear communication
- Misdirected communication

Let's break them down.

1. Over-Communication

Over-communication usually happens when clients are anxious. "They send updates constantly—every thought, every email, every screenshot, and occasionally a legal theory borrowed from someone who once watched a courtroom TV show."

One man once sent me nineteen emails in a single weekend. Nothing in his case had changed—he was simply thinking out loud. But every email required reading, sorting, and responding. His bill expanded significantly.

Put yourself in the lawyer's shoes. Suppose he brought you a shoebox of documents, in no particular order and without organization. Would it take you longer to sort and understand them than if organized and carefully indexed? If your lawyer charges $500 an hour, you are paying them more than $8 a minute to organize them for you. Ask yourself whether that is how you want your legal budget spent.

The cure for over-communication is to send one organized update instead of ten scattered ones, stick to facts, not feelings, and ask yourself: "Does this require action right now?"

2. Under-Communication

Under communication is just as dangerous—sometimes more so. Clients often assume lawyers know things automatically, or they forget to mention details that could completely change the direction of a case. I once had a client mention, three months into the case, that he had recorded a phone call with the opposing party. This wasn't a minor detail. It was the detail.

Missing information doesn't just slow a case—it warps strategy. Smart Clients share early, share fully, and share consistently.

3. Emotional Communication

- Emotions are normal
- Emotion-driven communication is expensive
- Anger produces long emails; fear produces frantic calls; frustration produces rambling texts

All of these cloud the facts, derail the strategy, and create expensive detours. The fastest way to stop emotional communication is with one simple question: "What do I need my lawyer to do with this information?" If the honest answer is "nothing," don't hit send. Cool off. Then send only what matters.

4. Unclear Communication

Lawyers can handle almost anything except confusion. Clients sometimes write messages like:

- "What do you think about the thing from yesterday?"
- "Call me. It's important."
- "See attached." (Followed by three unlabeled PDFs.)

Clear communication looks like:

- "Attached: Updated timeline through 11/3."
- "Here are my top three questions before the hearing."
- "Here are the documents the mediator requested."

The difference between a $50 email and a $300 email is almost always clarity.

5. Misdirected Communication

This is when clients assume the lawyer is the right person for every question. Examples:

- Tech issues ("How do I open this PDF?")
- Emotional processing ("I'm so angry right now…")
- Non-legal personal decisions ("Should I sell my car?")
- Family counseling ("My sister is furious. What do I say?")

Lawyers will help, but at $300–$1,000/hour, it's not cost-effective. Smart Clients keep non-legal issues outside the legal team. Lawyers should solve legal problems—not emotional ones, not technical ones, and definitely not family drama.

The Client Who Tried Hard (a Little Too Hard)

One client—a wonderful man, very kind—emailed me constantly with updates that had nothing to do with his case:

- His dog's surgery
- His neighbor's hedge
- His thoughts about the NFL draft
- A photo of a sandwich he really liked

He wasn't being difficult. He just needed a connection. But it slowed the case and inflated his bill. Once we established a clear rule—"legal updates only"—everything improved immediately.

It is common for lawyers to engage in meaningful conversations with their clients to build rapport, make clients comfortable with the relationship, and ensure new clients become long-term clients. Most lawyers do not record billable time for such conversations. But once the relationship is established, continued non-case conversation can quietly expand the bill unless clear boundaries are set.

I have tried to reserve such matters for the end of my calls and meetings, and I let the client know, "We are no longer on the clock." I might entertain a client at lunch or dinner and let the client know that, even if we discuss his or her case, no time will be billed unless we agree it is a working lunch or dinner.

The lawyer might let the client know early on that all time spent is billable unless otherwise stated. The Smart

Client might ask the lawyer to let them know when the clock starts and ends so as not to add to their bill. This can be delicate but wise. Also, at the beginning of the relationship, perhaps take notes on the length of calls or meetings, then look at the itemized bill and compare the lengths recorded. This might give a hint into how much social time is billed.

My twelve-hour-a-day practice was almost always a sprint and rarely a marathon. Five extra minutes spent discussing a client's weekend was five minutes removed from another client's urgent matter—or from my own family. Remember this, and you will protect both your time and your budget.

Communication isn't about volume—it's about precision. Smart Clients don't overwhelm their lawyers with noise or starve them of information. They send clear, concise, factual updates that move the case forward and nothing more.

When you master this skill, everything becomes easier. Your lawyer works faster. Your bills shrink. Your stress drops. And your case moves with purpose instead of confusion.

In the next chapter, you'll learn how to take this clarity one step further by building the systems and habits that keep your legal life organized even when things get emotional.

See Appendix A for templates and worksheets.

CHAPTER THIRTEEN:
HOW TO COMMUNICATE IN HIGH-STAKES MOMENTS

High-stakes moments in a legal case feel different. They land heavier. They disrupt your breathing. They sharpen your focus or scramble it entirely. This chapter teaches you how to recognize those moments instantly and communicate in a way that protects—not jeopardizes—your position. Smart Clients don't just stay calm under pressure. They learn to speak, knowing that a single sentence can shift the entire outcome.

"In the midst of chaos, there is also opportunity."—**Sun Tzu**.

High-stakes moments are the defining moments of a legal case. These are the hearings, the deadlines, the settlement calls, the surprise filings, and the sudden emails—the moments where a single sentence can cost thousands of dollars or change the direction of the entire dispute.

In everyday communication, mistakes can be inconvenient. In high-stakes legal communication, mistakes create consequences. Smart Clients know how to shift gears when the stakes rise. They slow down. They speak clearly. They stay measured. They become, for a moment, their most rational selves. They communicate like someone who understands the weight of the moment.

What Makes a Moment "High Stakes"?

A high-stakes moment usually has at least one of these:

- Money on the line
- Time pressure
- A legal deadline
- Emotional conflict
- A potential turning point
- A message from the opposing side
- A decision your lawyer must make today

If your stomach drops or your pulse spikes when you see it, odds are the stakes are high.

The Most Common Mistake Clients Make Under Pressure

- They react instead of respond.
- Reaction is immediate, emotional, and almost always counterproductive.

The Smartest Clients Learn to Buy Themselves Three Simple Things:

- Time (even a few minutes is enough)
- Clarity (separating emotion from fact)
- Direction (waiting for legal guidance)

The Three-Part High-Stakes Message

When something urgent happens, send your lawyer a message in this exact format:

- A summary of what happened (2–3 sentences max)
- The exact document attached (clearly labeled)
- One question: "What do you recommend?"

This eliminates chaos, preserves clarity, and gives your lawyer exactly what they need to take decisive action.

The Power of a Neutral Tone

In high-stakes moments, you must become the calmest person in the room—even if you don't feel calm. Your tone should be neutral, concise, factual, and unemotional. This isn't cold. It's strategic. Opposing lawyers often interpret calm as a sign of strength, panic as a sign of weakness. Calm signals control.

Words You Should Never Use in a High-Stakes Moment

- "I'm furious."
- "This is insane."
- "We need to fight."
- "They're lying."
- "I won't stand for this."
- "This is unacceptable."

These phrases inject emotion, weaken your leverage, and create written records that can haunt you later.

Judges, mediators, and opposing counsel all pay close attention to tone.

What to Say Instead

- "I received the attached letter today."
- "Here is my understanding—please confirm."
- "Is there any time pressure I should know about?"
- "Please advise on the appropriate response."

These statements show steadiness and respect for the lawyer's role.

The "Silence Strategy"

Sometimes the strongest move in a high-stakes moment is deliberate, strategic silence. Opposing lawyers often send aggressive messages hoping you'll react emotionally. They want you to panic, lash out, or reveal information you shouldn't. A moment of strategic silence creates pressure. It forces the other side to wonder. Smart Clients never respond directly to the opposing side. Everything routes through their lawyer, who understands timing and leverage far better.

Calm Changed Everything

I was representing a client from Japan seeking to purchase a business in Oregon. The negotiation had dragged on for months—tense, technical, and increasingly fragile. The price gap was the sticking point. My client had invested a great deal of time and money and foregone other opportunities. We had a full conference room, and the seller's counsel sat at the head of the table. In this final scheduled meeting, he opened his briefcase, pulled a single sheet of paper from it, and pushed it toward me. "This is our final offer, take it or leave it." I read it with no hint of emotion.

I met with my client in a side conference room. I told my client that I knew the seller was under a great deal of financial stress due to an expiring bank loan. We agreed to call the seller's bluff. I warned my client not to say anything or show any sign of anger.

We walked back into the conference room. I took the paper from the conference room table with the price on it, flipped it over, and wrote "We greatly appreciate your good faith and diligence. We wish you the best of luck in selling your company," and pushed it back to the seller's lawyer. The lawyer read it, passed it to his client, and, together with the seller's executive team, they rose and left.

My client did not react but bowed and wished them well. A half hour later, the seller's lawyer called me and offered a new price that my client accepted.

Because my client didn't respond emotionally, we retained strategic control. A half hour later, we secured a favorable agreement—an opportunity that would have vanished if we had reacted impulsively. My client's calm wasn't a weakness. It was power.

High stakes require low emotion. Smart Clients approach these moments the way surgeons approach the operating table: steady hands, controlled breathing, and absolute clarity about the next move. Their calm becomes a form of leverage—one that opposing counsel can feel.

The truth is simple: high-stakes communication isn't about the words you choose. It's about the discipline behind those words. It's the choice to pause before responding, to gather facts before reacting, and to speak with purpose rather than panic.

When every word matters, calm is not a mood. It is a strategy—a form of power. And in the tightest moments of a legal case, it can be the difference between seizing an opportunity and forfeiting it. Master this, and you won't just survive high-stakes moments. You'll control them. And there's a reason lawyers are trained to think this way.

CHAPTER FOURTEEN:

HOW LAWYERS THINK

If you've ever wondered why lawyers hesitate before answering simple questions, why they ask for documents instead of stories, or why they seem calm at moments when you feel like screaming, there's a reason. Lawyers are trained to think differently—not better, not colder, but through a disciplined mental framework shaped by risk, evidence, and strategy. Once you understand that framework, working with a lawyer becomes easier, communication becomes smoother, and your entire case becomes more predictable. This chapter gives you that decoder ring.

"Judge a man by his questions rather than his answers."—**Voltaire**.

You don't need a law degree to understand how lawyers think. But once you do understand it, you become a calmer, clearer, more effective client. Lawyers aren't mysterious creatures. They're disciplined thinkers—methodical, analytical, and relentlessly structured. They process information differently, not because they're smarter, but because they've been conditioned to see problems through a specific lens. Once you understand that lens, everything becomes easier: communication, strategy, negotiation, decision-making, and expectations.

So let's pull back the curtain.

Lawyers Think in Terms of Risk, Not Certainty

When you ask a lawyer, "Will we win?" they pause. Not because they don't know the case, but because the legal system punishes certainty. Lawyers think like statisticians:

- What's likely?
- What's unlikely?
- What could go wrong?

This isn't pessimism. It's professional survival. A good lawyer identifies risks early so you aren't blindsided later.

Lawyers Care Far More About Facts Than Feelings

Clients lead with emotion:

- "I'm right."
- "I'm angry."
- "This is unfair."

Lawyers lead with evidence: "Show me the documents." It's not that lawyers are cold; it's that emotion doesn't win cases. Evidence, timelines, and documented facts do.

Lawyers Break Everything Into Elements

Every legal issue, no matter how dramatic, has a checklist baked into it. For example, defamation requires: a false statement, publication, harm, and fault. Miss one, and the case collapses. This "element thinking" is why lawyers ask so many questions. They're building the legal blueprint of your case—one required element at a time.

Lawyers Always Think Two Moves Ahead

Clients see the problem. Lawyers see:

- the problem
- the likely response
- the counter-response
- and the strategic consequences

This is the quiet chess game behind every legal decision—always planning the move after the next move.

A client once demanded that we send an aggressive letter immediately. I said no—not because the letter was wrong, but because the timing would trigger a counterattack we weren't ready for. Waiting changed everything.

Lawyers Expect Documents—Not Stories

Clients often start with memory: "I think it was around June…" Lawyers start with proof: "Do you have the email?" In law, evidence outranks memory every single time. If you want to think like a lawyer, anchor everything to something that can be shown—not just said.

Lawyers Assume the Other Side Has Secrets

Lawyers never assume they know everything. They assume a document is missing, a witness will shift, or opposing counsel has a surprise. This isn't paranoia; it's disciplined preparation.

Lawyers Think in Terms of Leverage

Leverage isn't about who's morally right. It's about who has better timing, stronger evidence, more to lose, less emotional volatility, and a clearer strategy. Leverage predicts outcomes far more accurately than outrage ever will.

Lawyers Don't Chase the Perfect Case

Clients want perfection. Lawyers want an advantage. Great lawyers don't need every fact—just the right ones. They don't need every document—only the ones that move the legal needle. They don't need the whole story—just the legally relevant slice.

Lawyers Stay Calm Because Panic Is Expensive

When clients panic, they push for impulsive decisions. Lawyers are trained to slow down under pressure. Their calm isn't indifference—it's discipline. A calm lawyer protects you. A calm client helps the lawyer think.

Lawyers Don't Fear Conflict—They Manage It

Most people avoid conflict. Lawyers walk toward it. But they don't pick unnecessary fights. They choose battles deliberately—calibrated around timing, risk, and leverage.

The Lawyer Who Seemed Too Calm

A client once said about another lawyer at my firm, "She isn't emotional enough. Does she even care about my case?" I asked him, "Does she return your calls?" "Yes." "Does she explain things clearly?" "Yes." "Does she have a plan?" "Yes." "Then she cares. She's just thinking like a lawyer—not like a client."

Once he understood that, their communication improved, the case improved, and his stress dropped instantly.

You don't need to think like a lawyer—you only need to understand how lawyers think. Once you grasp their framework, everything becomes easier: the pace of the case, the questions they ask, the caution they show, the way they prioritize documents over emotion. You stop mistaking calm for indifference, or hesitation for weakness, or strategic silence for inaction.

You begin to see the patterns they see—the risks, the leverage points, the timing, the hidden opportunities. You start participating in your case rather than just reacting to it. And that shift alone makes you a more powerful, more effective client.

Understanding the legal mind doesn't turn you into a lawyer. It turns you into a partner—someone who can think collaboratively, communicate strategically, and help build the strongest case possible. And once you understand how lawyers think, the next lesson becomes unavoidable: cases rarely stay on the path you expect.

CHAPTER FIFTEEN:

WHY CASES CHANGE DIRECTION

Every legal case takes on a life of its own. Even when you think you understand the direction, the law has a way of shifting under your feet. Smart Clients don't get rattled when that happens—they're prepared for it. They understand that strategy isn't rigid; it evolves as information, timing, personalities, and pressure points evolve. This chapter shows you why cases change direction and how the most effective clients respond when the ground moves.

"*Life is a series of natural and spontaneous changes. Don't resist them—let reality be reality.*"—**Lao Tzu**. (A philosophy lawyers secretly agree with, though they'd never put it on a billboard.)

If legal cases were predictable, you wouldn't need a lawyer—you'd need a spreadsheet and a highlighter. But cases twist, stall, accelerate, collapse, resurrect, pivot, and occasionally sprint toward an outcome no one saw coming. The best lawyers in the world cannot promise a straight line. Why? Because cases evolve as new facts surface, people react, and opportunities shift. Smart Clients don't fear these changes. They anticipate them. They adapt to them. They understand that strategy is not a concrete slab—it's a living document.

Why Cases Change Direction

Five major forces cause cases to veer, pivot, stall, or accelerate unexpectedly:

1. New Information Appears

A previously unknown email surfaces. A witness alters their story. A document you didn't know existed becomes the linchpin. A date you thought was accurate suddenly isn't. In law, information is power—and when information shifts, power moves with it.

2. The Other Side Panics, Stalls, or Surprises

Legal puzzles often hinge on human behavior. Opponents may hire new counsel, panic, escalate unnecessarily, drag their feet, or file an unexpected motion. Each move reshapes the landscape.

3. Judges Create New Realities

Judges don't follow your emotional timeline—or your preferred pace—because they can't. They follow the law, the procedure, and their daily docket. A delayed ruling, a pointed question from the bench, or a procedural requirement can reroute a case overnight.

4. Settlement Windows Open and Close

Negotiation behaves like weather patterns—constantly shifting, rarely predictable, occasionally stormy, and sometimes perfect. Pressure builds, shifts, or clears. Smart lawyers strike when momentum appears—not when the client feels impatient.

5. Emotional Climate Shifts

- Anger rises
- Fear takes hold
- Exhaustion sets in
- Relief opens a window

Emotion is fuel—sometimes combustible, sometimes catalytic—and when one side's emotional temperature changes, the entire trajectory can shift.

How Smart Clients Adapt to These Shifts

Smart Clients don't cling to one perfect path. They remain flexible, informed, and steady. They understand that a changing strategy isn't a weakness—it's intelligence. Here's how they adapt:

1. They Ask the Right Question: "What Changed?"

This question grounds the conversation in facts—not fear. When clients understand why things shift, they stop resisting and start collaborating.

2. They Stay Open-Minded

Smart Clients don't marry one plan. They allow the lawyer to adjust the sails as the legal winds shift.

3. They Stay Flexible About Outcomes

Victory takes many forms. A wise client doesn't insist on a single cinematic ending—they accept the path that leads efficiently to peace, resolution, or closure.

4. They Control Their Emotions

A rigid, emotional client is expensive. A flexible, calm client is powerful. Adaptability isn't just helpful—it's strategic.

5. They Recognize Opportunity When It Appears

A case can feel stuck for months—then suddenly a door opens. Poor clients get angry that the door isn't "perfect." Smart Clients walk through it.

The Case That Took a Left Turn

A client hired me for what appeared to be a straightforward contract dispute. We prepared for litigation. Everything was lined up. Then—unexpectedly—opposing counsel quit. His replacement called me and said, "My client wants this done. Can we talk?" Within three weeks, we settled for more than we had expected. The client asked, "Why did everything suddenly shift?" I told him, "Because legal cases don't move according to your schedule. They move according to the schedules of information, emotion, leverage, and opportunity—forces no client controls.

Flexibility isn't weakness. Adaptation isn't surrender. The client who adapts quickly wins more often—and spends less.

One crucial lesson I learned over the decades is that the frictional costs of litigation can quickly exceed the amount the parties are battling over. Most clients assume incorrectly that if they win, the other party will pay their lawyer. Wrong. Only in limited categories of cases—usually defined by statute or contract—does the loser pay the winner's legal fees.

Let's assume you have one of those cases where the contract in dispute provides that the winner collects the winner's legal fees from the loser. Ninety-five percent of cases settle before trial, and those settlements rarely allow a party to recover its legal fees. Even though a client believes at the outset that they will never settle, the statistics show otherwise.

Assume you go to trial and win. The judge has the discretion to make an award of what the judge believes are reasonable attorney fees. That is very often less than what your lawyer charged you. That is not because your lawyer overcharged you—it is because judges seek a 'fair' outcome and, more often than not, believe it is fair for the winner to share in the pain of the legal battle.

And even if the judge awards fees, you still have to collect them—a process that can be as difficult as winning the case itself. Clients often assume the loser pays their lawyer. No! The winner must pay their own lawyer and recover the costs from the loser. If the loser does not have the money and the client cannot collect, the client ends up paying those legal fees. Some losers hide their assets, and the client has to pay their lawyer even more to collect what the judge awarded.

I obtained a judgment that included my client's legal fees, but the defendant was very elusive. I took a debtor's exam of the defendant, during which I asked him questions under oath about his assets and their locations. As expected, he claimed total poverty. That was a disappointing report I had to deliver to my client.

Then a breakthrough came from an unexpected place. One of my partners noticed that the defendant regularly attended Portland Trail Blazers games—sitting courtside, no less. These tickets are 'season tickets.' This means the holder pays for their tickets and has a very valuable option to renew each season. I obtained an order from the court allowing the sheriff to show up at the room where the season tickets were held for pickup (this was before digital tickets). The sheriff showed up on the very first day before the defendant had the chance to claim his tickets. The sheriff seized the whole season's worth of tickets and attached the renewal option. A cashier's check for the full amount of the judgment was hand-delivered to my office that afternoon, and the tickets were released to the defendant.

When you accept that cases shift, stall, accelerate, and detour, you stop fighting the current and start navigating it. Smart Clients adapt quickly, ask better questions, stay emotionally steady, and recognize opportunity even when it arrives wearing strange clothes. In a system driven by timing, information, and human behavior, adaptability is not just helpful—it's a competitive advantage.

Rigid clients spend more, suffer more, and struggle more. Flexible clients pay less, stress less, and win more. The smartest clients become partners in the strategy, not passengers on the ride.

In a world where legal cases rarely travel in straight lines, adaptability isn't just wisdom. It's power. And when cases change direction, the most challenging question is no longer "What's happening?"—it's "What do we do next?"

CHAPTER SIXTEEN:

THE ART OF LEGAL DECISION-MAKING

Legal decision-making feels uncomfortable because the stakes are real, the information is incomplete, and every option carries consequences. Most clients try to make legal decisions the same way they make everyday ones—quickly, emotionally, or reactively. But the smartest clients learn that legal choices require a different mindset: slower, more precise, calmer, and grounded in strategy rather than instinct. This chapter gives you the framework lawyers use so you can make decisions confidently instead of fearfully.

"In the middle of difficulty lies opportunity."—**Albert Einstein**. (A comforting reminder when every legal option feels like a trap door.)

Legal decision-making bears almost no resemblance to everyday decision-making. In ordinary life, choices are guided by preference: what you want to eat, where you want to travel, what color to paint the guest room. In the legal world, choices are guided by consequences—

financial, emotional, strategic, and sometimes life-altering.

Most clients make legal decisions with the same instincts they use for personal ones: emotion, fear, urgency, or pride. Smart Clients make decisions like investors, negotiators, and strategists.

Why Legal Decisions Feel So Difficult

Two simple truths explain the difficulty: (1) there is rarely a perfect option, and (2) every option carries real risk. In law, you don't choose between perfect and terrible. You choose between imperfect and strategically beneficial.

The Lawyer's Framework for Decisions

Lawyers rely on a four-part structure—a mental checklist—to guide every meaningful decision:

- What is the goal?
- What are the risks?
- What is the leverage?

- What is the timing?

Clients who adopt this framework make dramatically better choices—and fewer costly mistakes.

1. Clarify the Goal (Most Clients Skip This Step)

Before choosing anything, ask:

- What outcome matters most?
- What outcome matters least?
- Which outcome will matter in five years?

Your personal goal may be:

- saving money
- saving time
- protecting reputation
- reducing stress
- achieving complete closure

Your lawyer cannot choose wisely until you decide what matters.

2. Understand the Real Risks (Not the Imagined Ones)

There are two types of risk:

- Legal risk—grounded in law and evidence
- Emotional risk—grounded in fear and imagination

Most clients confuse the two. Legal risk can be measured. Emotional risk can be managed.

3. Leverage Determines Power—Not Who's "Right."

A client once told me, "But I'm right!" I agreed. Being right is helpful. Having leverage is better. Leverage can come from:

- stronger evidence
- better timing
- clearer documents
- a calm, rational mindset
- a more credible legal posture

When choosing between options, the smartest question is: "Which choice increases our leverage?"

4. Timing Is Its Own Strategy

In law, when you act matters almost as much as how you act. Sometimes the right move is immediate. Other times, waiting strengthens your position. A negotiation pushed too early can backfire. A demand sent too late can lose momentum. Smart Clients never push for timing based on impatience. They ask: "How does timing affect leverage?"

The Decision Triangle: A Simple Tool for Smart Clients

Every legal decision can be evaluated with three questions:

1. Does this move me closer to my goal?
2. Does this increase or decrease risk?
3. Does this strengthen or weaken leverage?

If a choice passes those three tests, it's usually the right one—even if it's not the emotionally satisfying one.

Emotional Decisions Are Expensive Decisions

Lawyers can always tell when a decision was made in anger, fear, panic, or pride. Those decisions generate:

- more conflict
- more filings
- more fees
- worse outcomes

Emotional satisfaction is fleeting. Legal consequences are durable.

A client once rejected a settlement offer because he was furious and wanted to "teach them a lesson." I told him the offer was strong and might be the best we'd see. He refused. Two months later, the opposing side uncovered a document that weakened our case. The offer vanished. The case dragged on for another year. He wasn't stubborn—he was human. He made a legal decision based on emotion instead of logic. The smartest clients understand that: timing + leverage = opportunity.

Legal decision-making isn't about comfort—it's about strategy. Smart Clients choose the option that advances the goal, minimizes risk, and strengthens leverage—even when it's not the option they *feel* like choosing.

There's an old saying in the legal profession: a good settlement is one where both sides walk away slightly dissatisfied—and thoroughly relieved.

The right legal decision is rarely the one that feels satisfying in the moment. It is the decision that moves you closer to your long-term goal with the least risk and the greatest leverage. Smart Clients learn to choose strategy over emotion, clarity over impulse, and progress over pride.

Legal decision-making isn't about finding the perfect path—it's about choosing the wisest next step. When you adopt the lawyer's framework, you stop making decisions out of fear and start making them out of strength. You become calmer, clearer, and far more effective.

In the end, good legal decisions aren't born from certainty. They're born from discipline. And once you master that discipline, the legal world becomes far less intimidating—and far more navigable. And once you learn to make disciplined decisions, the next challenge is sustaining those habits.

CHAPTER SEVENTEEN:

WHAT LAWYERS WISH EVERY CLIENT UNDERSTOOD FROM DAY ONE

Every lawyer has a silent wish list—the essential truths they hope every client understands before the first phone call, before the first meeting, and certainly before the first crisis. These aren't complaints or ego-driven demands. They're the insights that make cases smoother, cheaper, faster, and far less stressful for everyone involved. This chapter reveals those truths so you can begin your case not just informed, but ahead.

"Justice is a machine that, when someone has once given it the starting push, rolls on of itself."—**John Galsworthy**. (A poetic way of saying: once the legal process begins, it moves according to its own machinery—not your preferred pace.)

Every lawyer—regardless of style, specialty, or temperament—quietly wishes clients understood a handful of truths before the first meeting even begins. Not because lawyers are impatient or arrogant, but because these truths make the entire process smoother, faster, cheaper, and far less stressful for everyone involved.

This chapter pulls back the curtain on the mindsets and habits that consistently set the most successful clients apart from those who struggle unnecessarily.

The Law Is Slow—Even When Everyone Is Doing Their Job

Most clients assume delays reflect incompetence. Not true. The legal system is built on procedure, scheduling, documentation, and court availability. For instance, some courts require a mandatory 30-day response period before a motion can even be heard—meaning progress may be occurring even when nothing appears to be happening. Even the most efficient lawyer cannot outrun the structure within which they work. Patience isn't a luxury—it's part of the process.

Facts Matter More Than Feelings

Lawyers care about your feelings—the court, however, does not. In practice, actionable facts are what move a case forward.

What wins cases?

- emails
- documents
- contracts
- timelines
- witnesses

Feelings guide strategy. Facts determine outcomes.

Communication Must Be Clear, Concise, and Focused

Lawyers prioritize actionable facts. The more precise your communication, the faster your case moves—and the less you pay. Clients who communicate clearly save time, money, and frustration. Clarity is cost control.

Google and AI are Not Legal Strategies

Online horror stories, forum posts, and generic articles rarely mirror your actual situation. Every case has different facts, laws, judges, timelines, and people involved.

In 2023, a New York lawyer filed a legal brief that contained multiple case citations. The problem? None of the cases existed. They were invented—completely fabricated—by an AI program. The case, *Mata v. Avianca*, quickly became national news. The lawyer hadn't checked the citations. The judge did. What followed was painful: The lawyer had to stand before the court and admit he didn't know the cases were fake. The judge issued a written order explaining that the brief "referenced non-existent judicial opinions." The lawyer was sanctioned. His professional reputation took a public hit.

The lesson wasn't "don't use AI." The lesson was never to rely on unverified information—from anywhere. Lawyers are responsible for every word filed in court, no matter where it comes from. This case became the cautionary tale of the decade: AI can assist, but it cannot replace legal judgment—and it certainly cannot or shouldn't invent facts, evidence, or case law.

Legal strategy is handcrafted—never copied and pasted from the Internet. Don't hire a lawyer if you believe AI can do better, and AI will not charge you—and good luck with that!

Silence Doesn't Mean Nothing Is Happening

Most of your lawyer's real work is quiet work analyzing, drafting, negotiating, researching, and anticipating the other side's moves. Clients often mistake silence for inactivity—when, in reality, the most important legal work happens in the quiet. In fact, the quiet hours are the ones that win cases. Some of my most brilliant ideas for a client occurred while I was tossing and turning, sleep eluding me, or in my morning shower before the formal workday began. And in case you wondered, no, I did not charge my clients for sleeping or showering.

Your Lawyer Is on Your Side—and Needs Your Trust

Trust is not blind faith—it's strategic efficiency. It reduces friction, saves money, and accelerates good outcomes. When clients second-guess every recommendation, the case slows. When they trust the expertise they're paying for, strategy accelerates.

Your Decisions Shape the Case More Than You Realize

Clients often think lawyers control everything. In truth, clients control their goals, their documents, their communication, their deadlines, their emotional reactions, and their willingness to compromise. These choices influence outcomes as much as anything the lawyer does.

Aggression Isn't Strength—Strategy Is

Decades of legal research consistently show that aggressive lawyers achieve worse long-term results than their calmer, more organized peers. Studies found that highly adversarial lawyers—those who relied on intimidation, sharp tone, and constant conflict—produced worse long-term outcomes for their clients. Judges rated them as less credible. Opposing counsel dug in harder. Settlement windows closed. And juries, surprisingly, were less persuaded by displays of force and more persuaded by clarity, structure, and professional restraint.

Subsequent studies reinforced the same conclusion: the lawyers who consistently achieved the best results were not the loudest or most aggressive—they were the ones who remained calm under pressure, prepared meticulously, listened carefully, and communicated with precision. These lawyers built more trust with judges, negotiated more effectively, and avoided the emotional escalation that drives up fees and down outcomes. In other words, the legal system quietly rewards discipline, organization, and strategic thinking—traits that look "mild" on the surface but win cases in practice.

Truth Always Surfaces—So Be Completely Honest

Nothing derails a case faster than hidden facts. Lawyers wish every client understood they can work with any truth, but they cannot work with surprises. Honesty isn't merely ethical—it's strategic. Secrets cost clients money. Don't conceal facts from your lawyer that you feel will harm your case. You wouldn't do that with your doctor, and don't do it with your lawyer.

The Goal Is Resolution, Not Revenge

Revenge feels good for ten minutes. It's catastrophic for the next ten months. The real measure of a successful outcome is stability, closure, peace, and financial predictability. Revenge delivers none of those.

A man once labeled every message—email, letter, voicemail—as an emergency. Every single one. After months of this, I finally told him, "You don't have a legal emergency," I finally told him. "You have an urgency problem." Once he learned to distinguish actual emergencies from emotional ones, the case smoothed out. His decisions improved. His bill dropped. The entire tone of the dispute changed.

The lawyer-client relationship is a partnership—but the client sets the tone. Smart Clients understand how the system works, communicate with clarity, stay emotionally steady, and trust the expertise they're paying for.

When clients understand these truths early, everything changes. Cases move faster. Bills get smaller. Decisions get clearer. Stress levels drop. Moments that once felt chaotic begin to feel manageable—even strategic.

Understanding how the system works doesn't just make you easier to represent; it makes you more powerful within it.

CHAPTER EIGHTEEN:
HOW TO KEEP LEGAL COSTS LOW

"A lean case is a focused case."—**Janet Reno**.

Most clients assume legal costs rise because lawyers enjoy billing. The truth is far less dramatic—and far more helpful. Legal costs balloon when cases become inefficient, disorganized, overly emotional, or poorly communicated. A disciplined client can cut fees by 30–50% without sacrificing results. A chaotic client, meanwhile, unknowingly sponsors their lawyer's next snowboarding vacation.

Legal fees only *feel* mysterious. At their core, they're built on predictable structures that nearly every firm uses. The problem is that clients rarely know which structure they're stepping into—or how much control they actually have over the final bill.

This chapter gives you a clear roadmap. By the end of it, you'll understand:

- every significant type of legal fee

- how lawyers think about value
- what costs you can control
- the red flags that signal you're heading toward a billing disaster

Why Legal Fees Feel Confusing

Because most people hire a lawyer the same way they hire a plumber: something went wrong, they want it fixed, and the price feels like the worst part.

But legal billing is not like home repair. Law involves uncertainty—timelines shift, opposing counsel misbehaves, courts reschedule, and new facts appear. Lawyers must price a moving target. And clients, understandably, want a stationary bill.

Good lawyers try to be transparent. Smart Clients demand clarity. Most billing frustrations stem from mismatched expectations: clients want certainty, lawyers want flexibility, and the legal system offers neither.

The 5 Biggest Drivers of High Legal Costs

If you understand what actually drives a legal bill upward, you can prevent half of the damage before your lawyer ever touches their keyboard. Every lawyer sees the same patterns, year after year:

1. Disorganized documents
2. Emotional emails or calls
3. Repeating the same questions
4. Long, unfocused communication
5. Waiting until the last minute

Eliminate those, and your bill drops instantly—*sometimes dramatically.*

1. Organize Documents Like a Pro

"Few things drain attorney time—and inflate your bill—faster than searching for missing or mislabeled documents." The more documents your lawyer must search, the more hours you pay for.

Smart Clients:

- label files clearly
- keep everything in one digital folder
- avoid sending duplicates
- create a simple one-page timeline

These habits alone have saved clients thousands of dollars.

But organization isn't just about neat folders—it's about protecting the information that could win or lose your case. In an age where confidential documents travel at the speed of a click, Smart Clients insist on secure methods for sharing files with their lawyers. Email is convenient, but it is not always safe—and sending sensitive documents through unsecured channels can create real risks, including accidental disclosure or cyber-theft. A far better approach is to ask your lawyer to establish a secure client portal where documents can be uploaded, downloaded, stored, and organized in a protected environment.

Many law firms use professional-grade systems such as ShareFile, Box, NetDocuments, iManage, or industry-specific encrypted portals that allow clients to drag and drop files without worrying about who else might gain access. Smaller firms may choose reputable options such as Dropbox Business or Microsoft OneDrive (Business Edition), which offer multi-factor authentication, restricted sharing, and audit logs. These systems keep everything in one place, eliminate the chaos of buried email attachments, and reduce the risk of something important being lost—or worse, intercepted.

If your lawyer does not routinely use a secure portal, you can (and should) request one. A well-managed digital workspace helps both sides stay organized, shortens response times, reduces miscommunication, and provides a clear trail of what was shared and when. In a world where legal matters often turn on documentation, a secure portal is not a luxury; it is Smart Client practice.

Several years ago, a mid-sized construction company became the center of a lawsuit involving delayed payments and disputed change orders. The client regularly emailed documents to its lawyer—blueprints, updated contracts, internal memos, subcontractor statements—none of which were encrypted or organized. Everything came through email, often forwarded several times, sometimes from jobsite Wi-Fi networks or public hotspots.

One afternoon, the company's project manager accidentally sent the entire email chain—including confidential legal strategy, draft settlement positions, and internal notes—to the opposing party's accountant, whose email address auto-filled because it started with the same first name as the lawyer's paralegal. The accountant forwarded it to his client, who immediately turned it over to their lawyer. The damage was instant and catastrophic: the attorney–client privilege was waived for every document in the chain, and the opposing lawyer learned the company's bottom-line settlement number. "Internal weaknesses in the company's timeline were exposed, and a key factual admission—intended only for their lawyer—became an exhibit at the next hearing to torpedo a strong legal position." Digital sloppiness is not a minor inconvenience—it is a litigation hazard.

The judge called it "a self-inflicted evidentiary wound." The dispute, which should have been settled for a modest amount, ballooned into a six-figure judgment. All of it could have been avoided with a secure client portal.

A protected file system, such as ShareFile, Box, or NetDocuments, would have prevented the auto-fill mistake, avoided accidental forwarding, and kept privileged documents from leaking into the wild. Instead, the case became a textbook example of how informal document handling can destroy a strong legal position.

2. Use the One-Message Rule

Instead of five emails before lunch, send one organized message at day's end with:

- updates
- questions
- documents
- requested clarifications

- anything the lawyer needs to move the case forward

A single well-structured message is infinitely cheaper than a scattershot of panic-grams throughout the day. Your lawyer will thank you, and your invoice will, too.

3. Ask High-Quality Questions

Vague questions cost time. Specific questions save time. Instead of: "What should I do?" Try: "Here are the three options as I understand them—which aligns best with our strategy?" The second question gets you a fast, actionable answer. The first invites a 20-minute lecture. The second invites a two-sentence answer.

4. Don't Rush Unless It's Truly Urgent

Emergency work is expensive because your lawyer must drop other matters, reshuffle deadlines, and act immediately. Taking an ambulance to the hospital is much more expensive than driving to your doctor's office. Smart Clients learn the difference between real emergencies (court deadlines, new filings, time-sensitive opportunities) and emotional emergencies ("This email feels urgent"). Legal work done in calm conditions is cheaper and more accurate. More than once, a client has labeled a midnight email from their ex-spouse as an "emergency," only to discover the court didn't care—and the bill did. Emotional chaos is the most expensive fuel on earth.

5. Let Your Lawyer Drive Strategy

As I discussed earlier, when clients push a strategy based on emotion, costs explode. When strategy is driven by leverage, evidence, timing, and legal positioning, costs shrink. Question your lawyer respectfully—not reactively.

Use Meetings Wisely

A clear agenda saves hours. Before every call or meeting, list your questions, attach the relevant documents, identify your goal, and know what you need by the end of the conversation. A wandering 50-minute meeting is three times as expensive as a focused 20-minute one. Lawyers aren't charging for the pleasure of chatting—they're billing for the time it takes to redirect a meandering conversation back to the goal.

Stay Ahead of Deadlines

Late-night scrambles cost money. Rushed documents cost money—and usually create mistakes that cost even more. Last-minute crises cost money. Smart Clients send documents early and respond promptly, which gives their lawyer room to think—and keeps the case efficient.

A client once came to me on a tight budget. He couldn't afford mistakes—and he told me so directly. I taught him the one-message rule, the timeline method, and how to prepare for meetings efficiently. His legal fees were controlled. Not because he negotiated my rates, but because he removed inefficiency from the case.

6. A common problem with legal fees is the surprise factor.

If you expect a $5,000 bill and receive one, there is no issue. Instead, if you receive a $10,000 bill, that is a real problem.

Always ask your lawyer for a budget. The cost of litigation is notoriously unpredictable because your lawyer cannot predict the moves the opposition will make and the time it will take to address those moves. Don't accept that explanation. Your lawyer has handled many cases and will know what a case will typically cost. Ask your lawyer to break down the budget into phases of your case and the steps inside each phase. Phasing forces both you and your lawyer to think strategically rather than reactively. Have an understanding wth your lawyer that if it appears the budget is or will change, then an updated budget will be provided. One of my partners told his clients that he would call them if it appeared their budget would be exceeded by more than 10%. He found that very effective.

Clients are also often under the impression that if their case becomes too expensive to pursue that they can simply drop it, pay their legal fees, and walk away. It is usually a one-way road: if you try to walk away, you pay your lawyer, pay the other party's lawyer, and perhaps even pay for counterclaims brought by the other party. Litigation is easy to start, complicated to pause, and expensive to escape.

In the end, lowering your legal bill has nothing to do with fighting harder and everything to do with working smarter. Lawyers reward clients who are organized, focused, and strategic. Courts reward cases that are lean and disciplined. The more clarity you bring to the process, the less you spend—and the stronger your position becomes.

Keeping legal costs low isn't just about organization and communication—it's about knowing where cases are most often resolved. The vast majority of legal disputes don't end with a dramatic courtroom verdict; they end in negotiation, mediation, or settlement discussions where discipline, preparation, and emotional control matter most. This is where inefficient behavior becomes expensive, and where Smart Clients can protect both their legal position and their wallet at the same time. In the next chapter, we'll look at how to navigate mediation and settlement talks strategically—so you don't undermine months of careful work at the very moment resolution is within reach.

CHAPTER NINETEEN:
HOW TO SURVIVE AND THRIVE DURING MEDIATION, SETTLEMENT TALKS, AND NEGOTIATIONS

"A good settlement is better than a good lawsuit."—**Abraham Lincoln**. (Lincoln practiced law for decades and was famously in favor of peaceful resolution.)

Settlement Discussions

There is one step that should always precede mediation. That step is an informal settlement discussion, which is more efficient and less costly than mediation.

I represented a real estate broker until his death at age 100. He was quirky, with a small but loyal client base and a lifelong habit of stumbling forward and somehow getting things done when common sense said he shouldn't. He had a small office building with an open floor plan with two suites separated by a kitchen and bathroom. There was a single thermostat. He leased out one suite, and his business occupied the other. My client liked the offices warmer, and his tenant liked them cooler. They spent weeks sneaking to the thermostat when the other was not watching and adjusting it. This eventually escalated to the point where my client brought me in. We met and eventually agreed on a schedule for the day and the temperature to be set at each time interval. My client came in early, so the heat could be higher, and the other tenant came in late and worked late, so that the heat could be lower. What they were fighting over wasn't truly about temperature—it was about control. And like most disputes, it escalated not because the issue was big, but because no one knew how to de-escalate it.

Now the fun part. I knew these two would continue to needle each other by varying the temperature by a degree or two and then feigning innocence. I crafted, and they agreed to, the "Danish clause." Any future disputes would be resolved by binding arbitration. The Danish clause said that before one party could start arbitration, they had to buy a box of Danish, deliver it to the other party, and then sit down with the other party for 30 minutes over coffee and Danish to try to resolve the dispute before arbitration could start. They used the Danish clause twice, each time laughing more than arguing. By the third dispute, they didn't need the clause at all—they simply talked.

Never underestimate the power and effectiveness of a face-to-face meeting in resolving disputes, or the way a small ritual of humanity can repair a relationship. Most disputes don't need more law; they need more conversation.

Mediation

Mediation is a structured negotiation led by a neutral third party whose role is not to judge you but to help you reach a resolution. It's not about determining who's right; mediators don't issue rulings or punish anyone. Instead, mediation gives each side space to be heard, to understand the risks of litigation, and to explore solutions that a courtroom could never offer. Because the process is private, flexible, and controlled by the parties themselves, it often leads to faster, cheaper, and more creative resolutions than any judge could order.

I served as a mediator for the local circuit court for 15 years. Sharing the weaknesses I saw in each side's position was very effective in moving both sides toward a settlement. Settlement feels better than one party being crushed and the other having spent far too much money to recover far less than they think they deserve. A courtroom delivers a winner and a loser. Mediation aims for two survivors.

Most clients imagine mediation as a courtroom showdown without the judge—dramatic speeches, righteous arguments, and a final moment where the other side caves in awe of your moral superiority. In reality? Mediation is a business meeting wearing a tie, and, like any business meeting, the party that stays calm the longest usually does best. It's not about victory; it's about resolution—the kind that gives you back your time, money, and sanity. Smart Clients walk into mediation calm, prepared, and clear about what actually matters. They understand that negotiation is an art form built on patience, timing, and emotional discipline.

Why Mediation Matters So Much

Mediation is often the smartest path because it saves time, saves money, avoids risk, and produces certainty.

Court is unpredictable. Mediation gives you control over the terms, the structure, the timeline, and your future. Control is the one thing litigation reliably strips away; mediation hands some of it back.

The Biggest Mistake Clients Make

They walk in thinking mediation is about proving they're right. It isn't. Mediation is about crafting a deal that protects your long-term interests—even if it's not the cinematic triumph you imagined in your head.

Step One: Know Your True Goal

Before mediation, you must know:

- What outcome do I need?
- What outcome do I want?
- What outcome can I live with?

Confusing these three will derail a negotiation faster than any bad offer.

Step Two: Expect a Roller Coaster

Mediation follows a predictable emotional arc:

- Optimism
- Frustration
- Impasse
- Breakthrough
- Resolution

If you recognize the pattern, the low points won't shake you. Most "impasses" are really just the halftime show.

Step Three: Don't Get Hooked by the Opening Offer

The first offer is almost always ridiculous. It is supposed to be ridiculous. Opening offers are psychological anchors, not verdicts on your worth. Treat them like the sticker price on a used car—a starting point, not a prophecy.

Step Four: Let Your Lawyer Do the Heavy Lifting

Your lawyer knows how to frame your strengths, how to soften your weaknesses, how to create leverage, and how to read the mediator's subtle cues.

Clients who negotiate from emotion often sink the ship they're trying to steer. Trust your lawyer to navigate with strategy, not adrenaline.

Step Five: Manage Expectations

A settlement isn't carved from marble—it's a practical agreement designed to give you peace. If justice shows up, too, count it as a bonus. But the real goal is to walk away legally protected, financially stable, and emotionally lighter. Perfection is a fantasy. Peace is a gift.

Step Six: Use Silence as a Tool

Silence terrifies negotiators. When you stay quiet at the right moment, the other side often fills the space with information—or concessions. Stillness is not weakness. It is leverage disguised as calm.

Step Seven: Know When Enough Is Enough

Smart Clients know when the deal is good enough to take. You don't get extra points for dragging a negotiation across the finish line panting and victorious. You get points for ending it wisely. A settlement that gives you predictability, closure, protection from future litigation, and the ability to move forward is often better than a trial that might give you glory—or disaster.

In one mediation, both parties were within inches of agreement. Then my client leaned in and said, "I want one more thing." I pulled him aside and asked, "Do you want one more thing, or do you want this over?" He paused, exhaled, and said, "I want this over." Ten minutes later, the case was over. Months later, he told me it was the most peaceful night's sleep he'd had in years.

Mediation isn't about winning the moment—it's about winning back your life. A trial gives you a verdict. A settlement gives you freedom. And freedom, for most clients, is worth far more than whatever victory they imagined in their head.

Successful mediation and settlement outcomes rarely happen by accident. They're the result of clear goals, disciplined thinking, and careful preparation long before anyone sits down at a negotiating table. The calm, strategic choices that lead to resolution are usually forged in quieter moments—during strategy meetings where risks are assessed, options are weighed, and direction is set. The next chapter shows you how to prepare for those meetings like a professional, so your lawyer can think clearly, act decisively, and guide your case toward resolution instead of reaction.

CHAPTER TWENTY:

HOW TO PREPARE FOR YOUR LAWYER'S STRATEGY MEETING LIKE A PRO

Most clients walk into strategy meetings unprepared, anxious, and hoping their lawyer will magically pull clarity out of thin air. Smart Clients do the opposite: they arrive ready, focused, and organized. They treat the meeting like a professional briefing—because that's exactly what it is. (Unlike the DMV, this meeting actually has a purpose.)

"Give me six hours to chop down a tree, and I will spend the first four sharpening the axe." —**Abraham Lincoln**.

A strategy meeting is not a casual conversation. It is where major decisions are made, the next steps are defined, risks are assessed, and the trajectory of the case is set. Preparation changes everything.

Why Preparation Matters

Every minute your lawyer spends searching emails, re-explaining concepts, or deciphering three-paragraph text messages is a minute you are billed—and a minute not spent on strategy. Prepared clients save money, move faster, think more clearly, and help their lawyers make sharper decisions. Preparation isn't about impressing your lawyer—it's about equipping them with the raw materials needed to think, analyze, and strategize at a high level.

Step One: Bring a Clean, Updated Timeline

The timeline is the backbone of your case. It should be chronological, concise, factual, and supported by documents. A good timeline does about 40% of your lawyer's mental work for them. (The other 60% is fueled by caffeine and existential dread.)

Step Two: Identify Your Top Three Goals

Not ten. Not seven. Three. Ask yourself what outcomes matter most? What outcomes matter least? What will I regret in five years if I don't push for it now? When clients are clear about goals, strategy snaps into focus like a telescope turned the right way.

Step Three: List Your Biggest Fears

Smart Clients don't hide their fears; instead, they surface them. Instead, they write down their biggest concerns, the worst-case scenarios rattling around in their head, and any emotional landmines. Lawyers can't address fears they don't know exist.

Step Four: Gather All Relevant Documents in One Folder

Physical or digital doesn't matter. What matters is organization. Label everything clearly: "Contract–Final," "Email–March 17," "Photos–Incident," "Receipts–Repairs." A consolidated folder can save hours of legal billing—and prevent the dreaded 'Do you know where that document went?'" lull in a strategy meeting.

Step Five: Prepare High-Quality Questions

Instead of asking, “What should I do?” Try: “Here are the options as I understand them—which aligns with our goal?” “What are the biggest risks in pursuing Option A?” “How might the opposing side respond if we do X?” High-quality questions don’t just save time—they sharpen your lawyer’s thinking.

Before you finalize a strategy, you must know your personal red lines.

Step Six: Know Your Boundaries

This step is often overlooked—and crucial. Ask yourself: What am I unwilling to do? What am I unwilling to spend? What public exposure can I tolerate? Which compromises are acceptable? Your lawyer needs this to design a strategy that aligns with your real-world limits—not your ideal-world instincts. Boundaries prevent you from agreeing to something in the heat of the moment that you’ll resent once the adrenaline wears off.

Step Seven: Bring Calm Energy

Strategy meetings go sideways when clients arrive angry, overwhelmed, frantic, or emotionally overheated. Bring the calmest version of yourself. Calm creates clarity. Clarity creates strategy. You cannot out-strategize your own stress level.

Step Eight: Capture Everything

Smart Clients take notes—lots of notes. A strategy meeting is information-dense. You will forget details if you don't write them down. These notes will guide your communication, questions, and decisions moving forward.

Lawyers do not learn everything in law school, just as a college degree does not prepare you for life. It may give you a head start, but the real work lies ahead. I was handling my first significant business transaction and had a meeting with a lawyer from a very large and prestigious law firm in San Francisco. I came to the meeting with a file with documents punched in on both sides. To locate items, I had to thumb through the pages, find them, and take notes on what was needed and what was provided. He came to the meeting with a checklist of items and matching folders. As you might guess, he was immensely more productive than I was. I immediately learned from his example and revamped my approach. Checklists became my bible for every legal project, no matter the size, with corresponding file folders. This was a game-changer for me. I pass that hard-earned lesson along to you as a client. Checklists aren't just tools; they are discipline on paper. They keep complex matters from collapsing under their own weight.

Preparation isn't paperwork. Preparation is power. A well-prepared client gives their lawyer clarity, direction, and efficiency—three things that cannot be manufactured in the moment. When you walk into a strategy meeting organized and calm, you change the entire trajectory of the case before a single word is spoken.

Preparation gives your case structure—but it doesn't make the process short. Even the most organized and disciplined clients are often surprised by how emotionally demanding legal matters can become over time. Strategy meetings sharpen direction, but endurance is what carries you through the long stretches in between. That's why being a Smart Client isn't just about documents and decisions—it's about managing the psychological grind that legal battles impose. The next chapter focuses on that overlooked skill: how to protect your emotional health, maintain perspective, and stay steady when cases take longer, cost more, and test your patience more than you ever expected.

CHAPTER TWENTY-ONE:
HOW TO MANAGE THE EMOTIONAL GRIND OF A LONG LEGAL BATTLE

Lengthy legal battles don't just challenge your wallet—they challenge your nervous system, your patience, your relationships, and sometimes your identity.

"Endurance is not just the ability to bear a hard thing, but to turn it into glory."—**William Barclay**.

Lengthy legal battles wear people down not because they're complicated, but because they're endless. Weeks become months. Months become years. The emotional toll begins quietly, then grows louder: frustration, exhaustion, resentment, fear, and the steady erosion of patience. (If lawsuits came with frequent-flier miles, at least you'd get a vacation out of it.) Smart Clients understand that the psychological strain of a long case is just as real—and just as important—as any legal argument. This chapter gives you the tools to survive, and even thrive, during the long haul.

Why Long Legal Battles Are Emotionally Draining

Legal battles are marathons, not sprints. Emotional fatigue sets in because of uncertainty (which the brain hates), lack of closure (which prevents healing), repeated conflict (which keeps you in stress mode), financial pressure (which amplifies anxiety), and slow timelines (which make you feel trapped).

There is nothing wrong with you if the process drains you. It would drain anyone.

Step One: Build an Emotional Routine

You need a structure for your emotional health just as you do for your documents. Smart Clients create routines that include exercise, journaling, scheduled breaks from thinking about the case, social connection, and activities that spark joy and mental relief. Your brain performs better with predictable patterns.

To keep emotional overwhelm from turning into chaos, you need a system—and one of the most powerful systems I ever adopted was a simple checklist.

My checklist tool is ideal. I typically keep the checklist. It has a label for the project at the top and a key with shorthand abbreviations for each player, such as **S** for Seller, **B** for Buyer, **SA** for Seller's attorney, **BA** for Buyer's attorney, and others for other participants, such as lenders and title companies.

Then my first column is an item number (1, 2, 3, etc.). The second column lists the tasks to be completed (draft agreement, etc.). My third column lists which party has been assigned each task. My fourth column lists the due date for each task. The final column is for listing the task's status. I update it weekly and email it to my client so they stay up to date. This saves money because the client no longer needs to reach out to check the status. It has the added benefit of allowing the client to reach out to me if the status of a task is of heightened concern or has changed. Ask your lawyer to do this for you if your matter is complex. This will be a pressure valve release each time the updated checklist arrives. You also save money by not repeatedly contacting your lawyer to ask about the status of your case.

Structure reduces stress. Every checkbox you mark on the checklist is one less worry you have to carry in your head.

Step Two: Use the "Legal Compartment" Technique

This mental discipline prevents the case from taking over your life. This is how it works. Choose a specific daily time (15–30 minutes) to review updates or think about the case. Outside that window, redirect your mind elsewhere—deliberately. This protects your mental space and reduces constant rumination.

Step Three: Reduce Exposure to Conflict

Clients often fall into emotional traps: rereading hostile emails, imagining worst-case scenarios, replaying conversations, or obsessively checking documents. Limit your exposure. You don't need to relive conflict to resolve it.

Step Four: Understand the "Middle Phase" Slump

Every long case has a middle phase: motions crawl, deadlines extend, the other side stalls, and your energy dips. This phase feels awful—but it is temporary. The middle phase is where most frustration accumulates and where most regrettable decisions are made. Knowing it's coming takes away half its power. Smart Clients expect the slump and resist the urge to panic or force unnecessary action during it.

Step Five: Celebrate Small Wins

Momentum matters emotionally. Small wins can be: a document produced, a motion granted, a negotiation opening, a judge's helpful comment, or simply a moment of clarity in the chaos. Recognizing progress fuels endurance.

Step Six: Don't Go Through It Alone

Long cases isolate people. They withdraw, feel misunderstood, or stop sharing. Smart Clients maintain support systems: friends, family, therapists, and mentors. Talking isn't a weakness—it's maintenance. But choose your sounding board wisely: some people amplify stress, while others absorb it. Pick the absorbers.

Step Seven: Focus on What You Can Control

Legal systems move slowly. Opponents behave unpredictably. Judges have their own timelines. But you do control your preparation, communication habits, emotional discipline, expectations, and financial planning. Control creates emotional footing—a place to stand, even when the case feels unsteady.

Step Eight: Practice the "Five-Year Test"

Ask yourself: "Will this matter in five years?" Often, the answer is no—and that realization deflates 70% of short-term stress. This test doesn't minimize your struggle; it simply right-sizes your perspective.

And sometimes what clients need most is not legal advice but reassurance.

A woman once called me midway through a two-year case and said, "I don't think I can do this anymore." I told her, “That’s not failure—that’s the middle phase. It always feels worst right before a breakthrough.” Two months later, the case settled favorably. Her emotional endurance, not her legal position, carried her through the final stretch.

My experience is that clients rarely have the patience, money, or emotional endurance to survive a lengthy court battle. That is why 95% of civil cases settle. Unfortunately, this realization comes after tens of thousands, or even hundreds of thousands, of dollars have been spent on the battle. Clients are often better served by compromising earlier and for less than they believe they should, because the extra amount they’re fighting for is usually dwarfed by the additional legal fees required to pursue it.

Lengthy legal battles aren’t won with adrenaline. They’re won with steadiness, structure, and emotional discipline. The clients who endure—calmly, deliberately, patiently—are the ones who reach the finish line with their case intact and their sanity still in one piece.

Endurance does more than protect your sanity—it shapes how you show up in the relationship with your lawyer. Clients who manage their emotions communicate more clearly, make steadier decisions, and create space for trust to grow even when pressure is high. Over time, that trust becomes the quiet force that determines how efficiently a case moves, how boldly strategy is executed, and how much stress the process creates along the way. The next chapter explores that force directly: how the best clients build trust with their lawyers—and why that trust often matters more than any single legal tactic.

CHAPTER TWENTY-TWO:
HOW THE BEST CLIENTS BUILD TRUST WITH THEIR LAWYER

Every successful legal relationship rests on one foundation: trust—not blind obedience, not flattery, not fear, but genuine confidence in your lawyer's judgment and integrity.

"The best way to find out if you can trust somebody is to trust them."—**Ernest Hemingway**.

Trust is the invisible currency of every attorney–client relationship—the force multiplier that makes everything else work. When trust is strong, communication is smooth, strategy is clearer, decisions are faster, and the entire case becomes more efficient and far less expensive. When trust is weak, everything slows down. Fear creeps in, doubt expands, and the legal process becomes far more stressful than it ever needed to be.

The best clients—the ones whose cases move quickly, whose outcomes are strong, and whose bills stay reasonable—share a single habit: they build trust intentionally, not accidentally. (They don't rely on luck, charm, or a well-timed compliment about their lawyer's tie.)

Trust often begins with transparency around money—an area where clients are most vulnerable, and lawyers are most scrutinized. I had what I called the Nordstrom rule of billing. I would tell my clients that if they received my bill and were unsatisfied with it, to call me and I would remove the charges they felt were unfair. In forty-two years of practice, I had only one client who demanded that I waive the bill in full. I did, and we parted ways professionally and peacefully.

Another approach I had with new clients with smaller matters was to offer to do the work for a nominal fee ($100). I would tell the clients that if they liked the work and the way we worked together, I hoped they would call me the next time they needed help. This approach immediately puts clients at ease and generates tremendous trust and loyalty. Small gestures of good faith often create more trust than hours of formal meetings.

Trust deepens fastest during the challenging moments—the messy, chaotic stretches where courage matters more than polish. One of the most important lessons I drilled into junior associates was this: "Get into *the mud.*" When a case turns ugly—and every real case eventually does—the instinct is to retreat, create distance, and wait for the chaos to settle. That's a career-killer. In those moments, a lawyer has two choices: step into the storm or retreat and hope the debris misses them." Clients immediately recognize which path you take. Marching forward means you will get dirty. You will take hits. You will collect scars. But those scars become the receipts of trust. When a lawyer wades into the mud for a client—fully, visibly, without flinching—that client almost always becomes a client for life. It's uncomfortable, it draws fire from all sides, and it takes real backbone. But it is the only right way to practice. When the mud starts flying in your case, pay attention: does your lawyer step forward—or step away?

Why Trust Matters More Than Anything Else

Contrary to popular belief, lawyers don't need you to like them. They don't need praise, flattery, or homemade cookies—though most won't turn those down. What they do need is your trust. Trust creates honest communication, strategic clarity, faster decisions, fewer misunderstandings, and a unified front against the other side. When clients trust their lawyer, the lawyer can act decisively. When clients don't, every step becomes a negotiation—and not the strategic kind.

The Five Behaviors of Highly Trust-Building Clients

1. They Tell the Whole Truth Immediately

Not the curated truth. Not the flattering version. Not the version you hope is "close enough." The whole truth. Lawyers can handle ugly facts. What they cannot handle is surprise. The earlier your lawyer knows the reality, the better they can protect you.

2. They Keep Commitments (Even Small Ones)

Trust grows through simple reliability: sending documents on time, returning messages promptly, showing up prepared, and meeting deadlines without drama. These habits tell your lawyer, "You can count on me." Inconsistency forces lawyers into defensive mode; reliability invites collaboration. Reliability is the backbone of trust.

3. They Ask Questions Without Fear

Some clients feel embarrassed asking questions. The best clients don't. They ask openly, clearly, and without embarrassment. Lawyers don't judge clients for being confused. They judge clients for pretending not to be confused.

4. They Separate Emotion From Direction

Clients are human—emotions happen. But high-trust clients don't let those emotions issue commands. Instead of saying, "I'm furious—do something," they say, "I'm upset, but I want your recommendation before I act." That one shift demonstrates maturity, stability, and strategic discipline.

5. They Give Their Lawyer the Benefit of the Doubt

Lawyers juggle dozens of cases, court schedules, deadlines, and unannounced surprises from opposing counsel. Smart Clients assume workflow—not neglect. This mindset prevents pointless friction and strengthens the relationship.

What Trust Looks Like in Practice

Trust doesn't just feel nice—it creates measurable strategic advantages: Your lawyer works faster. Your lawyer communicates more candidly. Your lawyer can negotiate more aggressively. Your lawyer spends less time clarifying misunderstandings. Your lawyer can take calculated risks on your behalf. In short: trust is not emotional—it's tactical.

What Destroys Trust (Usually by Accident)

Withholding information, contradicting your own story, questioning every recommendation, sending mixed directions, making emotional demands, comparing your case to your cousin's divorce, or to something you skimmed on Reddit. These behaviors make lawyers hesitate—and hesitation weakens strategy.

Trust reveals its value most clearly in high-stakes moments.

I once represented a man in a complicated business dispute. He didn't always like my answers, but he trusted them. He stayed steady, communicated clearly, and let the strategy unfold rather than forcing it. Halfway through the case, the opposing side made a major mistake—one we were ready for because he followed the plan. We settled on terms far better than he'd imagined. He told me afterward, "I didn't always understand the moves, but I trusted you had a plan." His trust didn't just help the case—it strengthened the strategy itself.

Trust amplifies every strength in your case. It sharpens strategy, accelerates progress, lowers cost, and steadies you during the worst moments. When you trust your lawyer—and behave in ways that earn their trust in return—the entire legal process becomes more precise, faster, and far more effective. Trust doesn't just change the relationship; it changes the outcome.

Trust reveals its true value when things don't go perfectly. In fact, the strength of the attorney–client relationship is tested not in smooth moments, but in how both sides respond when something slips, misfires, or needs correction. Smart Clients understand that mistakes are not the end of a good relationship—they are often the moment when professionalism, accountability, and judgment become most visible. The next chapter looks at how to respond when your lawyer makes a mistake—calmly, strategically, and in a way that preserves both your case and the trust you've worked to build.

CHAPTER TWENTY-THREE:
WHAT TO DO WHEN YOUR LAWYER MAKES A MISTAKE

Mistakes in the legal world feel terrifying to clients—not because they're common, but because the stakes are high. A single error can look catastrophic from the outside. The truth is more nuanced: most mistakes are small, fixable, and far less consequential than they appear in the moment. What matters far more than the mistake itself is what happens next.

"To err is human; to correct it is professional."—**Anonymous legal proverb**.

Lawyers are human. They make mistakes—just like doctors, accountants, engineers, and anyone whose work involves judgment, deadlines, and a profession held together by law, stress, and caffeine. Most mistakes are minor, fixable, and part of the natural complexity of legal work. But how a client responds determines whether the case recovers smoothly or spirals into unnecessary cost, conflict, or panic. Smart Clients don't catastrophize; they stabilize.

My colleagues and I often acknowledged that we made mistakes almost daily. A word is misspelled or left out, an email is sent but never received, a document is misplaced, or a client request is missed. "For clients who never make mistakes, I applaud you—and I've never met you." Ninety-nine times out of a hundred, the mistake never appears again—or if it does, it's fixed as part of ordinary workflow. Also, don't go out of your way to point out every minor mistake; if it has no impact on your case, it makes your lawyer's job harder and accomplishes nothing. The mistake wasn't intentional, and pointing out minor errors that don't affect your case often burns goodwill without improving results.

First: Understand the Types of Lawyer Mistakes

Not all mistakes are equal. They fall into four categories:

1. Harmless Errors

Examples include: a typo in an email, a mislabeled document, and small scheduling confusion. These are routine and carry no meaningful consequence.

2. Minor Process Errors

Examples: forgetting to CC you on an email, misunderstanding a small detail, or something needing clarification. These are quickly fixed and rarely affect the case.

3. Moderate Strategic Errors

Examples: a filing done later than ideal, suboptimal timing in negotiations, and a misunderstood preference or goal. These can be corrected. They rarely jeopardize the entire case.

4. Serious Mistakes

Fortunately rare, but possible: missing a major deadline, giving incorrect legal advice, or failing to disclose a crucial document. These require immediate attention, transparency, and a solution-focused mindset. I had one such case in which the lawyer for the other side wrote a letter outlining all the weaknesses in his client's case. My first name was the same as the lawyer's client's insurance company lawyer's first name, and he or his staff ended up addressing the letter to me instead of to 'Randy' at the insurance company. It was catastrophic for him and ended the litigation immediately—likely with significant help from his malpractice carrier.

Step One: Stay Calm

Your reaction influences the result. A calm client allows the lawyer to think clearly and act quickly. Panic doesn't fix mistakes—clarity does. Smart Clients pause, breathe, and gather facts before reacting.

Step Two: Ask for Clarification (Not Confrontation)

Instead of: "You messed up!" Try: "Can you walk me through what happened and what it means for the case?" This invites explanation rather than defensiveness—and produces far better information.

Step Three: Listen to the Plan for Correction

Good lawyers immediately explain what happened, apologize, outline the impact, and propose a solution. If your lawyer already has a plan, give them room to execute it.

Step Four: Evaluate the Impact Without Emotion

Clients often assume the worst. But most mistakes are: temporary, repairable, and far less serious than they appear in the moment. Evaluate logically, not emotionally. Fear magnifies every flaw; facts shrink them back to size.

Step Five: Communicate Clearly About Your Concerns

Factual, calm language is your friend: “My concern is…” “How does this affect our timeline?” “What are our next steps?” “Is there anything I can do to help solve this?” Clarity accelerates correction.

Step Six: Watch for Accountability

A good lawyer: owns the mistake, explains it plainly, and outlines how it won't happen again. A bad lawyer blames others, obscures details, or minimizes the problem. Accountability is the difference between a stumble and a warning sign.

Step Seven: Decide Whether This Is a Pattern or a One-Off

Everyone makes one-off mistakes. Patterns are different. Ask: Is this recurring? Does it damage trust? Is the lawyer transparent? Is their strategy still sound? Most clients continue smoothly after a single misstep. Patterns require reevaluation.

Step Eight: Know When a Second Opinion Is Appropriate

If the mistake seems serious and you're unsure, a second opinion provides clarity. This isn't disloyalty—it's responsible decision-making.

Step Nine: Know When to Change Lawyers

Smart Clients change lawyers only when trust has broken beyond repair, communication has collapsed, mistakes are repeated, strategy consistently falters, or ethics feel compromised. Switching lawyers is serious—but sometimes necessary. The lawyer will often advise you that they must resign because you have a claim against them and that continuing the representation would create a conflict of interest. They may refer you to their malpractice carrier, which can assign counsel at no cost to you.

A client once pointed out that I misread a date buried deep in a thick stack of documents—an easy error when a '6' masquerades as an '8' and the formatting predates modern typography. He approached me calmly, asking for clarification instead of assuming the worst. We resolved it together within the hour. It had zero effect on the outcome. His measured response turned a potentially tense moment into a productive one—and ultimately strengthened our working relationship.

A lawyer's mistake is not a disaster—it is a moment that reveals honesty, accountability, and professional character. The best clients respond calmly, the best lawyers correct swiftly, and together they turn a stumble into a stronger partnership.

How you handle mistakes reveals your judgment—and that judgment becomes even more visible when you step into a courtroom. Clients who respond calmly, listen carefully, and trust their lawyer during setbacks are far better prepared for the scrutiny that comes with appearing before a judge. Court is where composure, discipline, and respect stop being abstract virtues and start shaping real outcomes. The next chapter shows you how to prepare for that moment—how to show up steady, credible, and aligned with your lawyer so you don't undo good strategy with avoidable missteps when it matters most.

CHAPTER TWENTY-FOUR:

HOW TO PREPARE FOR YOUR DAY IN COURT

Court is not where you perform; it's where you are evaluated. And the person evaluating you—the judge—notices far more than most clients realize.

"In courtrooms, facts speak louder than theatrics—and judges have excellent hearing."—**Judge Irving Younger**.

Your day in court is not just a legal moment—it's a psychological, emotional, and strategic moment. Many clients imagine court as something out of *A Few Good Men*: raised voices, dramatic revelations, someone shouting, "You can't handle the truth!" In reality, court is structured, methodical, and often surprisingly quiet. Judges are not looking for theatrics or emotion. Instead, they are looking for clarity, professionalism, and respect. Smart Clients understand how to present themselves in a way that strengthens their case rather than unintentionally weakening it.

Step One: Understand the Purpose of the Hearing

Most court appearances are not trials. They are hearings—short, focused events addressing one or two issues. Typical examples are motion hearings, status conferences, scheduling hearings, temporary orders, and procedural matters. Understanding why you are there shapes everything: your expectations, your demeanor, and what your lawyer needs from you. Confusion breeds anxiety; clarity breeds confidence.

Step Two: Know Exactly What Will Happen

Before the court date, ask your lawyer: What exactly is the purpose of this hearing? How long will it last? Will I need to speak? What will the other side say? What does the judge already know walking in? What are the best-case and worst-case outcomes? Information reduces fear—and prevents surprise adrenaline spikes.

Step Three: Dress Like You Respect the Process

You don't need designer clothes. You do need to look neat, calm, and respectful. Good choices are business casual, neutral colors, clean shoes, and minimal accessories. Bad choices are loud patterns, overly casual outfits, sunglasses on your head, and anything you'd wear to mow the lawn. Judges don't expect fashion—just respect.

Court is one of the few places where appearance still signals respect, and judges notice who understands that.

I recalled interviewing a law student who hoped to land a summer job with my AM Law 100 firm. He was from a top law school and had excellent grades. He came to the interview in jeans and a ski jacket. I struck his name from the list the moment he walked into the interview room. It showed a lack of respect for the process, and the interview was effectively over before it began.

Step Four: Know Your Role—You Are Not the Lawyer

Clients sometimes derail hearings by interrupting, reacting visibly, whispering loudly, shaking their heads, or trying to correct the record in real time. Your lawyer speaks for you. Your job is to stay composed. In a courtroom, composure is credibility.

Step Five: Master the Courtroom Body Language

Judges read people as easily as lawyers read contracts. They notice anxiety, anger, arrogance, and disrespect. Smart Clients: sit still, maintain a neutral expression, avoid eye-rolling, keep hands visible, and look at the judge when addressed. Your body language should say, "I am steady, respectful, and focused."

Step Six: Control Your Reactions to the Other Side

The other side may exaggerate, misstate facts, or outright lie. Expect it. Your reaction must be silent, steady, and controlled. You gain credibility by refusing to take their bait.

High-profile cases make this point better than any book. During his New York civil fraud trial, Donald Trump repeatedly interrupted testimony and made audible comments while seated at counsel table. The judge eventually stopped the proceedings, turned to Trump's attorney, and said, *"Control your client. This is not a political rally."*

It didn't change the underlying legal issues—but it absolutely shaped how the court perceived his credibility. A single reaction at the wrong moment can do more damage than a weak legal argument. The judge isn't just evaluating the facts—they're evaluating you.

Step Seven: If You Must Speak, Speak Carefully

If the judge addresses you, pause for one second, breathe, and answer calmly and directly. Good responses: "Yes, Your Honor." "No, Your Honor." "I understand." "I don't recall." "Could you repeat the question?" Bad responses: "This is ridiculous!" "That's not what happened!" "They're lying!" Any sentence starting with "Let me explain everything..." Less is more when you're standing in front of the bench. Judges reward clarity and punish rambling. A short, direct answer often carries more weight than a long, defensive explanation.

Step Eight: Debrief After the Hearing

Smart Clients schedule a short debrief after court. Ask your lawyer: What went well? What concerns you?

What are the next steps? What should I expect next? Court is not the finish line—it's a checkpoint. A debrief prevents misunderstandings and ensures the next phase of the case starts on an aligned footing rather than in confusion.

One of my favorite lawyer TV dramas is *Boston Legal.* In one episode, a client grew increasingly agitated as opposing counsel painted an unflattering picture of him. Finally, the client jumped up and shouted, "That's outrageous!" The judge glared over his glasses and said, *"Sir, if you speak again without permission, I will find you in contempt. Your lawyer knows how to object. You do not."* Alan Shore leaned over with his trademark calm and murmured, *"Please don't help me like that again."* The courtroom chuckled—but the warning was very real.

Courtroom success isn't just about what you say—it's about how you carry yourself while you say it. Judges form impressions quickly, and those impressions influence everything that follows. When you walk into court prepared, composed, respectful, and steady, you give your lawyer an enormous strategic advantage before a single word is spoken.

How you conduct yourself in court doesn't just influence the hearing you're attending—it often shapes what happens next. Judges form impressions, records are created, and decisions are preserved in ways that directly affect your options once a ruling is issued. Sometimes the outcome is favorable. Sometimes it isn't. And when it isn't, Smart Clients resist the instinct to react emotionally and instead evaluate their next move with discipline and perspective. The next chapter walks you through that moment—how to assess a disappointing ruling, understand whether an appeal makes sense, and decide what to do next without letting frustration drive the strategy.

CHAPTER TWENTY-FIVE:
HOW TO NAVIGATE APPEALS

Few moments in the legal process hit harder than losing—whether the loss is small, procedural, or catastrophic. But the moment after the ruling is when Smart Clients separate emotion from strategy.

"The appellate court does not retry cases—it reviews them."—**Justice Benjamin Cardozo**.

Losing in court—or receiving a disappointing ruling—hits hard. Clients often feel shock, anger, disbelief, or the overwhelming instinct to shout, "We're appealing!" But appeals are not do-overs. They are not second chances to reargue your case. They are highly technical reviews with narrow questions and strict rules. Smart Clients step back, breathe, and understand the appellate landscape before making any decisions. Think of it like flying a plane: you don't pull the eject lever just because *you hit turbulence.*

Step One: Understand What an Appeal Actually Is

An appeal is *not* a new trial, a chance to introduce new evidence, a reevaluation of witness credibility, or an opportunity to convince a new judge that your side "felt" right. An appeal is a review of whether the lower court committed a legal error, based solely on the existing record, and evaluated by judges who were not present at the original hearing.

The appellate question is not "Who was right?" It is "Did the judge follow the law?" It is a legal audit, not an emotional rerun.

Step Two: Give Yourself Time to Process the Outcome

The moments after a ruling are emotional. Smart Clients do not make major decisions under the influence of adrenaline. Take a breath. Take a beat. Decisions made in calm thought are always better than decisions made in shock. Give yourself the grace of time before demanding action.

Step Three: Ask Your Lawyer for a Clear Explanation

Before thinking about an appeal, ask your lawyer: Why did the judge rule this way? What was the legal reasoning? Which facts mattered most?" Did the judge signal any concerns or limitations? Understanding the ruling is essential to making the right next decision.

Step Four: Evaluate Whether an Appeal Is Realistic

Not every loss is appealable. Many rulings fall within the judge's discretionary authority. Appeals succeed only when there is a clear legal error, a misapplied rule, an abuse of discretion, a constitutional issue, or something inconsistent with established law. Your lawyer will tell you whether the issue is legal or simply disappointing. Disappointment is not grounds for appeal. Legal error is.

Step Five: Understand the Cost and Timeline

Appeals are slow. Often 9–18 months. Sometimes longer. They are also more expensive than most clients expect because of transcript preparation, record assembly, extensive legal research, and the meticulous drafting required for appellate briefs. Smart Clients consider whether the emotional and financial investment matches the potential reward.

Step Six: Consider the Probability of Success

Appellate courts overturn trial rulings far less often than clients imagine. A serious conversation with your lawyer might cover the likelihood of success, the strength of your legal arguments, similar appellate cases, and tendencies of the appellate panel. Emotion shouldn't guide the decision. Believe it or not, appellate courts have personalities—some panels lean conservative, others liberal, some deferential, others interventionist. Your lawyer will know the difference.

A perfect example is the appeal Alex Jones filed after the Sandy Hook defamation trial. His legal team raised a long list of complaints—claims of judicial bias, evidentiary errors, and unfair limits on his defense. The Connecticut Supreme Court rejected every argument. Why? Because appeals don't replay the drama of a trial, they scrutinize the law applied in the trial. And the trial judge had followed the rules. The decision wasn't overturned because the outcome wasn't about emotion, controversy, or public pressure—it was about whether a legal error occurred. It hadn't. His case is a reminder that even massive verdicts, national attention, and aggressive appellate arguments rarely move the needle unless the lower court truly got the law wrong.

Step Seven: Explore Alternatives

Sometimes the best response to a bad ruling isn't an appeal. Options may include negotiation, settlement, modification, compliance with minimal disruption, or a broader strategic shift. An appeal is one tool among many—not the default reaction. An innovative pivot can outperform a high-risk appeal.

Step Eight: If You Appeal, Prepare for a Very Different Process

Appeals involve written arguments, precisely formatted briefs, strict deadlines, and occasionally short oral arguments. Your appellate attorney becomes part legal scholar, part expert writer—not a courtroom performer.

Step Nine: Manage Your Emotional Expectations

Appeals feel distant and slow. There are no dramatic moments or surprise witnesses. Just long stretches of silence followed by dense legal documents. This quiet period is normal, not a sign that anything is wrong. Often, your trial lawyer will advise you that they are a trial lawyer but do not handle appeals. You may be referred to a lawyer who handles appeals exclusively. That lawyer will undoubtedly meet the Surgeon or Schoolteacher archetype. Appellate work rewards precision, order, and intellectual discipline—exactly what those archetypes excel at.

Appeals often feel urgent, but urgency is almost always emotional, not strategic. A client once lost a motion hearing and immediately insisted, “We’re appealing. This judge is wrong.” I asked for one week. One week to let emotions settle. During that time, his anger faded. We reviewed the ruling together. The judge’s reasoning was solid. An appeal had almost no chance. Instead of appealing, we pivoted—and used the ruling to open a new negotiation window. Three weeks later, we settled the case on terms far better than anything an appeal would have offered. Feeling wronged is emotional. Navigating the next step is strategic.

Even though your opposition defeated you in the trial court, they are very likely upset and angry at the prospect of being back in court for another two or three years on appeal and paying their lawyer even more legal fees. This creates an excellent incentive for settlement. As a lawyer, I often filed a notice of appeal (with a short deadline) to preserve rights and signal seriousness. That filing alone frequently triggered settlement conversations—opponents dread years of additional litigation just as much as you do.

Appeals require precision, patience, and perspective. Smart Clients evaluate their options calmly, understand the narrow purpose of appellate review, and make decisions based on strategy rather than emotion. An appeal can be powerful—but only when it aligns with the law, the odds, the cost, and your long-term goals.

Appeals force clients to confront a difficult truth: not every fight is worth continuing. Even when an appeal is legally possible, the more critical question is often whether it serves your life, not just your case. Smart Clients learn to distinguish between preserving rights and prolonging conflict, between strategic persistence and emotional inertia. And once that distinction becomes clear, a different challenge emerges—not how to keep going, but how to finish well. The next chapter of this book focuses on that moment: how to close a case with clarity, reclaim your sense of self, and step forward without letting a legal dispute define what comes next.

APPEAL-READINESS CHECKLIST FOR CLIENTS

☐ Have I received a written explanation of the ruling?

☐ Do I understand the legal error we are alleging?

☐ Have I reviewed the cost and timeline of an appeal?

☐ Have I evaluated whether the appeal is financially worthwhile?

☐ Does my lawyer believe the odds justify the effort?

☐ Do I understand what the appellate court can—and cannot—fix?

☐ Have I gathered all prior filings and transcripts?

☐ Have I accepted that an appeal is not a second trial?

CHAPTER TWENTY-SIX:
HOW TO FINISH YOUR CASE STRONG

The end of a legal case isn't just the conclusion of a dispute—it's the moment you take control of what comes next, and that transition deserves as much intention as any legal strategy.

"The end of a legal case is not a victory lap. It's a doorway back into your life."—**Former Chief Justice Margaret Marshall**.

The end of a legal case rarely feels like the movies. There is no swelling music, no dramatic applause, and no moment where everything suddenly feels resolved. Most endings feel quieter—sometimes anticlimactic, sometimes confusing, sometimes deeply bittersweet. Smart Clients understand that the conclusion of a case is not just a legal event; it's a life transition. How you navigate that transition shapes your financial stability, emotional recovery, and long-term peace.

Step One: Get Complete Clarity on the Final Outcome

Before the file closes, sit down with your lawyer and review exactly what the ruling or settlement says, what obligations you still have, any deadlines that apply, which documents require signatures, and what (if any) future risks remain. Finishing strong means finishing informed. Ambiguity is stressful; clarity is freedom. Clients often assume the case ends when the judge speaks—but the real ending happens when every obligation is understood and completed.

Step Two: Understand Your Responsibilities—Fully

Most cases end with action items: payments, transfers, or reimbursements; filings or registration updates; compliance obligations; behavioral guidelines (in family cases); and follow-up deadlines. Smart Clients create a checklist, mark deadlines, and complete tasks promptly. Loose ends generate anxiety now and legal problems later.

Step Three: Resist the Urge to Re-Fight the Past

After a case ends, many clients replay the conflict: "We should've pushed harder." "They didn't deserve that outcome." "Why didn't this turn out differently?" These thoughts are understandable—but they are emotional quicksand, pulling you backward into a fight that has already been decided. The past is decided; your power lies in what you choose to build next.

Step Four: Look for the Lessons, Not the Regrets

Every legal ordeal—even the painful ones—teaches something: how to protect yourself, how to communicate more clearly, how to choose relationships or partners more wisely, how to maintain documentation, how to set boundaries, and how to plan ahead. Lessons build resilience. Regrets build resentment. A case that costs you energy, money, or peace should at least repay you in wisdom.

Step Five: Rebuild Your Emotional and Mental Space

Lengthy legal battles drain energy in ways clients rarely notice until the case is over. Smart Clients rebuild by restoring routines, reconnecting with people they withdrew from, restarting healthy habits, taking a genuine break, and creating new goals unrelated to the case. Recovery isn't indulgence—it's essential maintenance for your mind and life.

Step Six: Secure Your Future with Proper Documentation

Depending on the case, closing the loop may include updating your will, trust, or beneficiary forms; modifying business agreements; adjusting financial protections; strengthening record-keeping; and formalizing boundaries in writing. Smart Clients fortify the future so they never face the same conflict again.

Step Seven: Close the Lawyer–Client Relationship Properly

A good closing conversation includes a case debrief, confirmation of all remaining steps, a summary of what to expect in the coming months, and guidance on preventing future disputes. This is the time to ask: "Is there anything I should do in the next year to protect myself?" The case may be over, but your life is not static. Good advice now prevents new problems later.

Before fully closing your file, understand that the end of a case often brings its own unique emotional and financial tensions.

There is a predictable—and professionally perilous—collision point between lawyer and client after a loss. During trial, the lawyer pours enormous time, judgment, and stamina into the case, but the bill for that effort typically lands only after the verdict. The client, already reeling from the emotional and financial impact of an adverse ruling, is then confronted with the largest invoice of the entire case. To a client, it feels like a second blow—first the loss, then the bill. To a lawyer, it is simply the unavoidable cost of the trial phase. This is the moment when blame looks for a home—and the lawyer is the only available address. A client cannot argue with the jury, confront the judge, or scold the opposing counsel, so the only remaining target is the lawyer. This is how fee disputes are born, how invoices get questioned, and how some clients simply disappear. Trial lawyers know this dynamic well; it's older than the profession itself. This is why proactive communication matters. When a client is regularly updated on trial budgeting—for example, knowing in advance that the trial phase is estimated at $60,000 and the final bill aligns with that—the collision softens, expectations stay grounded, and trust survives the verdict. Preparation doesn't just manage expectations—it preserves relationships.

Step Eight: Reclaim Your Identity Outside the Conflict

Legal battles can take over your identity. They shape your routines, thoughts, conversations, and self-perception. Finishing strong means taking back the parts of yourself that have been overshadowed—your hobbies, your relationships, your joy, your ambitions, and your peace. You are not your case. You are the person who endured it—and you get to decide who you become after it.

One client told me after a long case, "I feel like I've been holding my breath for two years." We made a closing plan—financial, emotional, and practical. Two months later, he emailed me: "I feel like myself again." The case didn't change. He did. That feeling—the return of self—is the real finish line.

Finishing a case is not an ending—it is an intentional beginning. A legal victory without personal closure is incomplete. A settlement without understanding is fragile. A case that ends without a transition plan leaves emotional debris in its wake. Smart Clients finish strong, finish organized, and finish with clarity about the life they are stepping back into. The case is over—now your next chapter begins.

Finishing a case well doesn't mean you'll never need a lawyer again—it means you're better prepared if you do. One of the most important protections you carry forward into every future legal conversation isn't emotional resilience or organization, but confidentiality. What you say to a lawyer, when you say it, and how you protect that information can shape outcomes long before a dispute ever reaches a courtroom. That's why the next chapter turns to a topic many clients misunderstand, but every lawyer relies on: the attorney–client privilege—what it protects, how it's lost, and how Smart Clients use it to safeguard themselves long after one case has ended.

CHAPTER TWENTY-SEVEN: THE ATTORNEY–CLIENT PRIVILEGE—WHAT STAYS IN THE VAULT

Attorney–client privilege is one of the most misunderstood concepts in the legal world—and one of the most important protections a client has. Thanks to TV dramas, it's also one of the most mythologized.

"The attorney–client privilege is the oldest of the privileges for confidential communications known to the common law."—**Justice Thurgood Marshall**. (That elegant line has been quoted in more courtrooms, textbooks, and nervous first meetings than any client ever realizes.)

If lawyer–client communication had a theme song, it would be something dramatic—Mission Impossible, perhaps, but with fewer explosions and substantially more paperwork. The attorney–client privilege is the legal equivalent of a vault door: once you tell your lawyer something in confidence, the law generally locks it down. This privilege exists so clients can speak openly—about the good, the bad, the embarrassing, and the 'please don't tell my mother'—without worrying that their own words will later be used against them.

But let's get this out of the way: the privilege is not a magic cloak. It won't rescue you from loud voices, thin walls, or your own inability to use an inside voice. It doesn't protect conversations held loudly at Starbucks, discussions with your lawyer's neighbor, or anything you post on social media (looking at you, Facebook philosophers). It covers confidential communications made for the purpose of obtaining legal advice. That means if you confess your secret chili recipe to your lawyer, it's safe—though your lawyer may start wondering what kind of legal matter involves cumin and regret.

One of the biggest surprises for clients is discovering that the privilege belongs to them, not the lawyer. You own the lock. The lawyer holds the keys and prays you don't fling them into a crowd. That means you have the power to keep the vault locked or open it. Lawyers, on the other hand, are sworn to protect your confidences even if you'd prefer they didn't. (Clients sometimes want lawyers to 'just tell the judge what I said,' not realizing this is like asking a priest to livestream confessions.)

The privilege has limits. It does not shield plans for future crimes. If you're telling your lawyer how you previously purchased a questionable item on eBay, that's likely privileged. But if you're asking your lawyer the optimal way to ship illegal fireworks across state lines—congratulations, you've detonated the privilege. Lawyers call this the crime-fraud exception. Clients call it 'Wait… what do you mean I can't ask that?'

Handled correctly, the attorney–client privilege is one of the most powerful protections available to everyday people. It encourages honesty, fosters trust, and keeps your lawyer from being blindsided in court. So use it wisely: speak openly, ask questions, and remember that your lawyer can only protect the secrets they actually know.

Here's where people accidentally blow holes in their own privilege without meaning to. When I took depositions, I would ask the other party whether they had ever shared any advice their lawyer had given them with anyone else. There was often stuttering and sputtering by them and their lawyer; ultimately, they had to answer, and out came the cats, the kittens, and the occasional mountain lion.

A recent, headline-grabbing example of attorney–client privilege being pushed to its limits came from the federal investigation into classified documents stored at former President Donald Trump's Florida residence. Prosecutors sought testimony from Trump's lawyer, Evan Corcoran, arguing that specific conversations fell under the crime-fraud exception. This narrow rule removes privilege when legal advice is used to further a crime. A federal judge reviewed Corcoran's private notes and ordered him to testify about specific conversations with his own client. Many were stunned, mainly because they assumed 'privilege' meant 'unbreakable. The case became a national reminder that the privilege is powerful, but not indestructible—and when a client crosses certain legal boundaries, the vault door can swing wide open.

And please—for the sake of everyone involved—don't test the limits of the privilege on social media. Your lawyer can defend a lot of things, but not screenshots or Instagram posts.

Understanding attorney–client privilege—what it protects, how it's lost, and how easily it can be compromised—is one of the final pieces of becoming a truly Smart Client. But principles only matter if they hold up in the real world, when pressure is high, and decisions have consequences. To bring everything together, the final chapter walks through a real-life case from start to finish, showing how preparation, communication, budgeting discipline, emotional control, trust, and confidentiality work together when it actually counts. This is what the Smart Client Mindset looks like in motion.

CHAPTER TWENTY-EIGHT:
A SMART CLIENT CASE STUDY—FROM CRISIS TO RESOLUTION

When most people picture hiring a lawyer, they imagine dramatic courtroom fireworks or midnight war-room meetings. In reality, most legal matters start quietly, with something that feels small but unsettling. That's exactly how it began for Sarah Whitmore, a Portland small-business owner who woke up one Tuesday to find a former contractor had filed a construction lien claiming she owed him $38,000 for "unpaid development work." Sarah believed the work was incomplete, the invoice inflated, and the threat of litigation outrageous. More importantly, she understood that liens don't disappear on their own—they harden. She knew ignoring a construction lien was how minor problems become five-figure ones.

Step One: Deciding Whether She Really Needed a Lawyer

Sarah didn't panic. She opened her Smart Client notebook (yes—she actually made one) and walked through the guidance in the book.

- Is the issue legal in nature? Yes.
- Is there potential financial or reputational risk? Definitely.
- Is the opposing party represented? Not yet, but the filed lien suggested it was on the way.

This was no longer a DIY problem. It was lawyer time.

Step Two: Finding the Right Lawyer (Instead of the Closest One)

Instead of Googling "business lawyer near me" and hoping for the best, Sarah used the hiring checklist from the book:

1. Ask three trusted business colleagues for referrals.
2. Review each lawyer's website for clarity, transparency, and professionalism.
3. Schedule short consultations and ask the "Smart Client Questions," including:

- "How would you budget this matter?"
- "What are potential off-ramps before litigation?"
- "What's your preferred communication protocol?"
- "How do you avoid surprise billing?"

What the checklist didn't tell her was which lawyer would treat her like a partner instead of a problem—but the conversations did. Two lawyers mainly spoke about their own brilliance. One listened carefully, explained his plan rather than the maze, and offered a practical plan. Sarah hired the third.

Step Three: Aligning Expectations and Setting the Rules of Engagement

Before signing anything, Sarah requested:

- A written budget range
- A flat-fee option for a letter response

- An agreement that no task costing more than $1,000 would move forward without her explicit approval
- A secure portal (ShareFile) for all documents and messages

The lawyer readily agreed—relief point number one.

Step Four: The Work Begins

The lawyer reviewed the contract, emails, development drafts, and the whole project timeline. Using the secure portal kept everything in one place, eliminated lost threads, and prevented miscommunication.

He drafted a crisp, fact-focused response letter rejecting the contractor's inflated lien and documenting the incomplete work. No threats, no chest pounding—just a clean statement of facts supported by evidence. Two weeks later, the contractor escalated by hiring his own attorney.

Step Five: The Moment Everything Could Have Gone Sideways

The opposing lawyer sent an aggressive letter demanding payment plus attorney fees. This is where many clients panic and immediately cave. Not Sarah. She stuck to Smart Client protocol:

- Don’t respond emotionally—ever
- Ask your lawyer for options, not predictions
- Stay focused on strategy, not theatrics

Instead of predicting outcomes, she framed the decision in terms of cost, control, and risk. Her lawyer outlined three paths:

1. Settlement with a discount (fast but expensive)
2. Mediation (structured and predictable)
3. Prepare for litigation (slow and costly, but winnable)

Sarah chose mediation—controlled, efficient, and ripe for defusing nonsense.

Step Six: Mediation and the Power of Preparation

At mediation, the contractor arrived with a binder that looked impressive until it became clear it contained mostly screenshots and frustration. Sarah's lawyer arrived with a timeline, evidence of incomplete work, comparable billing rates, and a calm, professional demeanor.

The mediator quickly realized which side had the facts. Mediators don't take sides, but they know when one party is holding a real hand, and the other is holding receipts from the Internet. Momentum shifted. By lunch, the contractor's $38,000 demand had dropped to $20,000. By 3 p.m., he accepted $4,500 to walk away. Sarah paid it—not because she owed it, but because it cost less than fighting nonsense. Her attorney's fees were less than $3,000 thanks to budgeting guardrails and a flat-fee component.

Step Seven: The Aftermath

When it was over, Sarah told her lawyer: "I feel like I took an Uber through a legal storm I never could've driven through myself." She kept her business, her sanity, her budget, and her confidence. And most importantly, she learned that being a Smart Client doesn't mean knowing the law. It means knowing how to work with a lawyer.

A client who chooses the right lawyer, sets expectations early, demands transparency, uses secure communication, and stays strategic rather than emotional will always spend less money, reduce stress, and get better results.

This is what The Smart Client is all about. Not making you a lawyer—just making you the kind of client every good lawyer wants to have, and the sort of client bad lawyers hope never walks through their door.

CONCLUSION:
THE SMART CLIENT MINDSET

You may have started this book wanting to understand how to work better with lawyers—how to feel more confident, more prepared, and more in control. But somewhere along the way, you gained something bigger: a mindset. A way of thinking that protects you not just in legal matters, but everywhere decisions, conflict, and consequences intersect.

Once you see the system through this lens, you never see it the same way again.

The Smart Client Mindset isn't about memorizing statutes or speaking like a lawyer. It's the opposite: it frees you from believing you need to become one. It's about clarity, strength, preparation, organized thinking, emotional steadiness, and the confidence to advocate for yourself with purpose and respect. It's a way of approaching both the legal system—and your life—with intention instead of fear.

What You Now Know

You now know how to choose the right lawyer for the job. You know how to communicate clearly and efficiently. You understand how strategy evolves, how documents matter, and how timing shapes outcomes. You know how to behave in court, how to approach mediation, how to respond to mistakes, and how to evaluate an appeal with realism instead of adrenaline. You also know when to fight, when to negotiate, and when to step aside and let the process do its job.

Most importantly, you now know how to protect your legal, emotional, and financial future. This knowledge is not theoretical. It is practical power.

What the Smart Client Understands

Smart Clients don't blindly trust the system—and they don't fear it either. They understand how decisions get made, how lawyers think and prioritize, how cases grow, stall, pivot, and resolve, how to stay centered when conflict intensifies, and how to rebuild momentum when a case ends. This awareness becomes a kind of quiet armor—unflashy, unshakable, and always accessible. Unlike a court ruling, this power belongs exclusively to you. And once you experience this shift, you'll handle future legal challenges with a different kind of calm.

Your Legal Life Going Forward

You will face legal questions in the future—everyone does. A contract dispute. A real estate snag. A business disagreement that needs a steady hand. Perhaps a bankruptcy issue. Maybe a business problem. Maybe a family matter that requires careful navigation. Possibly something unexpected that lands on your desk without warning. But now, you will not face these moments blindly or anxiously. You will approach them with a mindset shaped by preparation, structure, and calm decision-making. You will ask better questions. You will choose more wisely. You will communicate more effectively. You'll partner with your lawyer rather than feeling dragged along by the process. That is the difference between surviving a legal challenge and steering it.

Years after a difficult case ended, a former client told me, "I used to think lawyers were something I had to fear. Now I feel like I know how to work with them—and how to stay in control of my choices." That is the moment every lawyer hopes for—not because the client becomes dependent, but because the client becomes empowered. Empowered clients make better decisions, spend less money, and walk away with far fewer scars.

Your Next Chapter

Your next legal chapter—whenever it comes—will be different now. You have tools. You're no longer guessing how the system works—you're navigating it. You have clarity. You have a playbook. You have the Smart Client Mindset. Carry it forward. Use it wisely. And remember, you can navigate any legal challenge with confidence, clarity, and composure—not because the system is simple, but because you are prepared.

A Final Story

Fresh out of law school, I never imagined this would happen, but when my formal legal career ended, some of my dearest and closest friends were clients. These were people who became friends first and clients second. They trusted me to do right by them, and I trusted them to be honest with me as I worked for them. It was a perfect partnership. I'm not suggesting every lawyer will become a lifelong friend. That's rare. But it can happen because of the closeness of the work, the shared battles, and the need for unqualified trust on both sides. Those friendships were the true reward—far beyond the legal fees that allowed me to support my family. If this book helps create more partnerships like those—built on trust, clarity, and shared purpose—then it has done its job.

Legal cases test people at their most vulnerable. They expose fear, uncertainty, and the limits of control. But they also reveal something else: the power of preparation, clarity, and disciplined choice. You cannot control every twist in a legal case—but you can decide how you show up, how you communicate, and how you decide what comes next. That is the Smart Client mindset. Carry it forward. Use it early. Use it deliberately. And long after this case ends, let it guide how you protect your time, your money, and your peace.

APPENDIX A:

SMART CLIENT TOOLS & FORMS

The following tools and worksheets help you put the Smart Client Mindset into action. You've learned how to communicate, prepare, strategize, and manage your lawyer effectively—these forms turn that knowledge into real-world practice.

FORM 1: ONE-PAGE CASE TIMELINE TEMPLATE

Case Name / Issue:

____

Your Lawyer: ____________________________________

Updated On: _________________ __, 20__.

Chronological Timeline of Key Events

List only major events or documents that affect strategy, deadlines, or decisions.

Date | Event / Action | Evidence / Document

________ | ___________________________ | ___________________________

________ | ___________________________ | ___________________________

________ | ___________________________ | ___________________________

Key Notes:

____

____

FORM 2: WEEKLY CLIENT UPDATE

Week of: ______________________ Case Name: ______________________

1. Summary of Developments This Week (Facts Only):

____

____

2. Documents Attached (label clearly and number in order):

____

____

3. Questions for My Lawyer:

1. ____
2. ____
3. ____

4. Information or clarification I need from my lawyer (be specific):

____

5. Upcoming Deadlines or Actions:

FORM 3: HIGH-STAKES MOMENT MESSAGE

Subject Line: [URGENT: New Document Received—Need Guidance]

1. Summary of What Happened (2–3 sentences):

____

____

2. Document Attached:
Name of file: ________________________________

3. My Question:
"What do you recommend as the next step?"
(Keep it to one straightforward question. Save other issues for a separate message.)

FORM 4: MEDIATION PREPARATION WORKSHEET

Case Name: ______________________________

Mediation Date: ________________ __, 20___.

1. What I NEED (non-negotiable):

____

2. What I WANT (ideal):

____

3. What I Can LIVE WITH (realistic outcomes I won't regret later):

____

4. My FEARS / Concerns (Name the specific pressure points you expect the other side to exploit):

____

5. My BIG PICTURE Goals:

____

6. Questions for My Lawyer Before Mediation:

1. ______________________________________
2. ______________________________________
3. ______________________________________

FORM 5: STRATEGY MEETING PREPARATION SHEET

Meeting Date: ________________,__, 20___.

Case Name: ____________________________

Purpose of meeting (e.g., settlement planning, motion strategy, budgeting):

____

____

1. Updated Timeline Attached: YES / NO

2. Documents I Am Bringing:

____

3. My Top Three Goals:

1. ________________________
2. ________________________
3. ________________________

4. My Biggest Concerns:

____

5. Questions I Want Answered:

1. ____
2. ____
3. ____

6. Boundaries:

Financial limits: ____________________________

Time constraints: ___________________________

Outcomes I cannot accept (deal-breakers):

____

FORM 6: SMART CLIENT CASE EVALUATION SHEET

Decision Being Considered:

(Use this sheet before any major decision—settlement, filing, deadline response, or negotiation shift.)

____

1. Does this move me closer to my goal?

☐ Yes ☐ No Why?

____

2. Does this move increase or decrease legal or financial risk?

☐ Increase ☐ Decrease: Explanation:

____

3. Does this strengthen or weaken leverage?

☐ Strengthen ☐ Weaken How?

____

4. Likely response from the other side:

____

5. What would my lawyer likely say?

____

6. If I do nothing, what happens?

____

FORM 7: BEST APPS FOR WORKING WITH YOUR LAWYER

Working with a lawyer today isn't just about meetings, phone calls, and long email chains. The modern Smart Client uses digital tools to streamline communication, securely store documents, track deadlines, and stay in control of their legal matter. The following ten apps are not only useful—they can save you time, money, and stress by making your interactions with your lawyer more organized and efficient.

1. *Clio for Clients*–Many law firms use Clio to manage cases. The client-facing app lets you upload documents, message your lawyer securely, review bills, check tasks, and see upcoming deadlines. If your lawyer offers access, download it immediately. It eliminates the mystery of "What's happening in my case?"

2. *Dropbox*–A simple, reliable file-sharing tool used by millions. Create a dedicated shared folder with your lawyer (if they allow it) for exchanging documents. It prevents lost attachments, version confusion, and the

risk of emailing sensitive information through unsecured channels.

3. *ShareFile*–A higher-security alternative preferred by many law firms. It allows encrypted document transfer and client portals. Upload PDFs, photos, or anything else your lawyer requests. It's one of the easiest ways to keep your case organized and protected from cyber risk.

4. *Scanner Pro*–Lawyers love clean, legible PDFs. This app turns your phone into a document scanner, complete with cropping, light correction, and automatic PDF creation—no more blurry photos of contracts on a kitchen table.

5. *Evernote*–An excellent app for organizing notes from meetings, phone calls, deadlines, and reminders. Create one dedicated notebook titled 'Legal' and keep everything in it. Tag items (like "deadlines," "questions," or "to discuss") and walk into every meeting prepared.

6. *Microsoft OneDrive*–Ideal for clients already using Microsoft 365. Stores documents securely, syncs across

devices, and works beautifully if your lawyer also uses Microsoft's ecosystem. Great for maintaining a tidy, cloud-based legal folder.

7. *Adobe Acrobat Reader*–Essential for reading, signing, and annotating PDFs. Lawyers send a LOT of PDFs. With this app, you can highlight, comment on, or sign documents digitally without printing.

8. *Calendly*–If your lawyer allows scheduling through Calendly, use it. It eliminates back-and-forth emails and lets you book meetings automatically based on their real-time availability.

9. *Google Calendar*–Critical for tracking your own legal deadlines, hearings, and appointments. Set reminders and alerts. Clients lose rights and leverage every day because they miss deadlines. Don't be that client.

10. *Signal*–A secure messaging app for situations where privacy is essential. Some lawyers allow clients to communicate through Signal for added confidentiality beyond standard texting or email. Just make sure only

to include your lawyer and, for the love of privacy, don't repeat Pete Hegseth's mistake of adding outsiders to a confidential thread.

Becoming a Smart Client means using tools that make your lawyer's job easier—and your case stronger. Tools don't replace judgment, but they dramatically improve it. These ten apps help you stay informed, stay organized, and stay ahead. In legal matters, preparation and clarity can be worth thousands of dollars. With the right apps, you're not just a client—you're an empowered partner in your own legal journey.

FORM 8: SMART CLIENT LAWYER SELECTION WORKSHEET

Use this worksheet before hiring a lawyer—and bring it with you to interviews.

PART ONE: DEFINE YOUR PROBLEM (BEFORE YOU MEET ANY LAWYER)

1. Briefly describe your legal issue (facts only—no emotions):

____

____

____

____

2. What type of matter is this? (check one):

☐ Litigation / lawsuit

☐ Business / contract

☐ Real estate

☐ Family / estate

☐ Personal injury

☐ Employment

☐ Other: ____________________

3. What is your primary goal? (check one):

☐ Win at all costs

☐ Minimize financial damage

☐ Resolve quickly

☐ Preserve relationships

☐ Reduce stress and uncertainty

☐ Other: ____________________

4. What matters most five years from now?

____

____

PART TWO: IDENTIFY THE RIGHT LAWYER TYPE

5. Which lawyer style best fits your situation?

☐ Shark—aggressive, forceful, pressure-driven

☐ Surgeon—precise, strategic, efficient

☐ Schoolteacher—patient, explanatory, steady

☐ Not sure yet

6. Why does this style fit your case?

____

____

PART THREE: INTERVIEW SCORECARD (USE FOR EACH LAWYER)

Lawyer Name / Firm:
____

Date Interviewed: ______________________________

A. Strategy & Judgment (Rate 1–5)

Understood my goals clearly 1 2 3 4 5

Explained risks honestly 1 2 3 4 5

Discussed strategy, not guarantees 1 2 3 4 5

Notes:

____

____

B. Communication Style

Listened without interrupting 1 2 3 4 5

Explained things clearly 1 2 3 4 5

Matched my communication needs 1 2 3 4 5

Notes:

____

____

C. Professional Signals (check all that apply)

☐ Asked smart questions

☐ Was prepared

☐ Did not badmouth other lawyers

☐ Discussed conflicts clearly

☐ Treated my matter seriously

Concerns (if any):

____

____

PART FOUR: FEES & STRUCTURE

7. Billing method discussed:

☐ Hourly

☐ Flat fee

☐ Contingency

☐ Hybrid

8. Did the lawyer explain what drives cost?

☐ Yes ☐ No

9. Did they explain what you can do to control fees?

☐ Yes ☐ No

Red flags noticed:

____

____

PART FIVE: YOUR INSTINCT CHECK

10. Did I feel pressured to hire immediately?

☐ Yes ☐ No

11. Did the lawyer promise outcomes?

☐ Yes ☐ No

12. Did I feel heard and respected?

☐ Yes ☐ No

13. Could I imagine working with this person during a stressful year?

☐ Yes ☐ No

PART SIX: FINAL DECISION SNAPSHOT

Strengths of this lawyer:

____

____

Concerns or weaknesses:

____

____

Overall fit for my goals:

☐ Excellent

☐ Acceptable

☐ Poor

SMART CLIENT REMINDER:

You are not choosing the "best lawyer." You are choosing the right lawyer for your problem, your goals, and your tolerance for cost, conflict, and stress.

www.ingramcontent.com/pod-product-compliance
Lightning Source LLC
LaVergne TN
LVHW050940210926
848482LV00013B/687
9798994288801